W9-APZ-704

FOURTH EDITION

Python
Pocket Reference

Mark Lutz

Beijing · Cambridge · Farnham · Köln · Sebastopol · Tokyo

Python Pocket Reference, Fourth Edition
by Mark Lutz

Copyright © 2010 Mark Lutz. All rights reserved.
Printed in Canada.

Published by O'Reilly Media, Inc., 1005 Gravenstein Highway North, Sebastopol, CA 95472.

O'Reilly books may be purchased for educational, business, or sales promo-
tional use. Online editions are also available for most titles (*http://my.safari
booksonline.com*). For more information, contact our corporate/institutional
sales department: (800) 998-9938 or *corporate@oreilly.com*.

Editor: Julie Steele
Production Editor: Sumita Mukherji
Proofreader: Kiel Van Horn
Indexer: John Bickelhaupt
Cover Designer: Karen Montgomery
Interior Designer: David Futato

Printing History:

October 1998:	First Edition.
January 2002:	Second Edition.
February 2005:	Third Edition.
October 2009:	Fourth Edition.

ISBN: 978-0-596-15808-8

[TM]   [2011-04-01]

1302022283

Contents

Python Pocket Reference

Introduction

Python is a general-purpose, object-oriented, and open source computer programming language. It is commonly used for both standalone programs and scripting applications in a wide variety of domains, by hundreds of thousands of developers.

Python is designed to optimize developer productivity, software quality, program portability, and component integration. Python programs run on most platforms in common use, including mainframes and supercomputers, Unix and Linux, Windows and Macintosh, Java and .NET, and more.

This *pocket reference* summarizes Python types and statements, special method names, built-in functions and exceptions, commonly used standard library modules, and other prominent Python tools. It is intended to serve as a concise reference tool for developers and is designed to be a companion to other books that provide tutorials, code examples, and other learning materials.

This *fourth edition* covers both Python versions 3.0 and 2.6, and later releases in the 3.X and 2.X lines. This edition is focused primarily on Python 3.0, but also documents differences in Python 2.6, and so applies to both versions. It has been thoroughly updated for recent language and library changes and expanded for new language tools and topics.

This edition also incorporates notes about prominent enhancements in the imminent Python 3.1 release, which is intended to subsume Python 3.0 (in this book, Python 3.0 generally refers to the language variations introduced by 3.0 but present in the entire 3.X line). Much of this edition applies to earlier Python releases as well, with the exception of recent language extensions.

Conventions

The following conventions are used in this book:

[ ]
> Items in brackets are usually optional. The exceptions are those cases where brackets are part of Python's syntax.

*
> Something followed by an asterisk can be repeated zero or more times.

a | *b*
> Items separated by a bar are often alternatives.

Italic
> Used for filenames and URLs and to highlight new terms.

`Constant width`
> Used for code, commands, and command-line options, and to indicate the names of modules, functions, attributes, variables, and methods.

`Constant width italic`
> Used for replaceable parameter names in command syntax.

Using Code Examples

This book is here to help you get your job done. In general, you may use the code in this book in your programs and documentation. You do not need to contact us for permission unless you're reproducing a significant portion of the code. For example, writing a program that uses several chunks of code from this book does not require permission. Selling or distributing a CD-ROM of examples from O'Reilly books does require permission. Answering a question by citing this book and quoting example code does not require permission. Incorporating a significant amount of example code from this book into your product's documentation does require permission.

We appreciate, but do not require, attribution. An attribution usually includes the title, author, publisher, and ISBN. For example: "*Python Pocket Reference*, Fourth Edition, by Mark Lutz. Copyright 2010 Mark Lutz, 978-0-596-15808-8."

If you feel your use of code examples falls outside fair use or the permission given above, feel free to contact us at *permissions@oreilly.com*.

Safari® Books Online

Safari® Books Online is an on-demand digital library that lets you easily search over 7,500 technology and creative reference books and videos to find the answers you need quickly.

With a subscription, you can read any page and watch any video from our library online. Read books on your cell phone and mobile devices. Access new titles before they are available for print, and get exclusive access to manuscripts in development and post feedback for the authors. Copy and paste code samples, organize your favorites, download chapters, bookmark key sections, create notes, print out pages, and benefit from tons of other time-saving features.

O'Reilly Media has uploaded this book to the Safari® Books Online service. To have full digital access to this book and others on similar topics from O'Reilly and other publishers, sign up for free at *http://my.safaribooksonline.com*.

Command-Line Options

Command lines are used to launch Python programs from a system shell prompt. Command-line options intended for Python itself appear before the specification of the program code to be run. Options intended for the code to be run appear after the program specification. Command lines have the following format:

```
python [option*]
  [ scriptfilename | -c command | -m module | - ] [arg*]
```

Python Options

-b

Issues warnings for calling `str()` with a `bytes` or `bytearray` object, and comparing a `bytes` or `bytearray` with a `str`. Option `-bb` issues errors instead.

-B

Do not write *.pyc* or *.pyo* byte-code files on imports.

-d

Turns on parser debugging output (for developers of the Python core).

-E

Ignores Python environment variables described ahead (such as `PYTHONPATH`).

-h

Prints help message and exit.

-i

> Enters interactive mode after executing a script. Useful for postmortem debugging.

-O

> Optimizes generated byte-code (create and use *.pyo* byte-code files). Currently yields a minor performance improvement.

-OO

> Operates like -O, the previous option, but also removes docstrings from byte-code.

-s

> Do not add the user site directory to the sys.path module search path.

-S

> Do not imply "import site" on initialization.

-u

> Forces *stdout* and *stderr* to be unbuffered and binary.

-v

> Prints a message each time a module is initialized, showing the place from which it is loaded; repeats this flag for more verbose output.

-V

> Prints Python version number and exit.

-W *arg*

> Functions as warning control; arg takes the form *action:message:category:module:lineno*. See warnings module documentation in the Python Library Reference manual (available at *http://www.python.org/doc/*).

-x

> Skips first line of source, allowing use of non-Unix forms of #!cmd.

Program Specification

scriptfilename

> Denotes the name of a Python scriptfile to execute as the main, topmost file of a program execute (e.g., `python main.py`). The script's name is made available in `sys.argv[0]`.

`-c` *command*

> Specifies a Python command (as a string) to execute (e.g., `python -c "print('spam' * 8)"` runs a print call). `sys.argv[0]` is set to `-c`.

`-m` *module*

> Runs library module as a script: searches for module on `sys.path`, and runs it as a top-level file (e.g., `python -m profile` runs the Python profiler located in a standard library directory). `sys.argv[0]` is set to the module's full path name.

`-`

> Reads Python commands from *stdin* (the default); enters interactive mode if *stdin* is a tty (interactive device). `sys.argv[0]` is set to -.

arg*

> Indicates that anything else on the command line is passed to the scriptfile or command (and appears in the built-in list of strings `sys.argv[1:]`).

If no *scriptfilename*, *command*, or *module* is given, Python enters interactive mode, reading commands from *stdin* (and using GNU readline, if installed, for input).

Besides using traditional command lines at a system shell prompt, you can also generally start Python programs by clicking their filenames in a file explorer GUI, by calling functions in the Python/C API, by using program launch menu options in IDEs such as IDLE, Komodo, Eclipse, NetBeans, and so on.

Python 2.6 does not support the -b option, which is related to Python 3.0's string type changes. It supports additional options:

- -t issues warnings for inconsistent mixtures of tabs and spaces in indentation (-tt issues errors instead). Python 3.0 always treats such mixtures as syntax errors.

- -Q division-related options: -Qold (the default), -Qwarn, -Qwarnall, and –Qnew. These are subsumed by the new true division behavior of Python 3.0.

- -3 issues warnings about any Python 3.X incompatibilities in code.

Environment Variables

Environment variables are system-wide settings that span programs and are used for global configuration.

Operational Variables

PYTHONPATH

Augments the default search path for imported module files. The format is the same as the shell's PATH setting: directory pathnames separated by colons (semicolons on Windows). On module imports, Python searches for the corresponding file or directory in each listed directory, from left to right. Merged into sys.path.

PYTHONSTARTUP

If set to the name of a readable file, the Python commands in that file are executed before the first prompt is displayed in interactive mode.

PYTHONHOME
> If set, the value is used as an alternate prefix directory for
> library modules (or `sys.prefix`, `sys.exec_prefix`). The
> default module search path uses `sys.prefix/lib`.

PYTHONCASEOK
> If set, ignores case in import statements (on Windows).

PYTHONIOENCODING
> *encodingname*[:*errorhandler*] override used for `stdin`,
> `stdout`, and `stderr` streams.

Command-Line Option Variables

PYTHONDEBUG
> If nonempty, same as -d option.

PYTHONDONTWRITEBYTECODE
> If nonempty, same as -B option.

PYTHONINSPECT
> If nonempty, same as -i option.

PYTHONNOUSERSITE
> If nonempty, same as -s option.

PYTHONOPTIMIZE
> If nonempty, same as -O option.

PYTHONUNBUFFERED
> If nonempty, same as -u option.

PYTHONVERBOSE
> If nonempty, same as -v option.

Built-in Types and Operators

Operators and Precedence

Table 1 lists Python's expression operators. Operators in the
lower cells of this table have higher precedence (i.e., bind
tighter) when used in mixed-operator expressions without
parentheses.

Table 1. Python 3.0 expression operators and precedence

Operator	Description
yield X	Generator function send( ) protocol
lambda args: expr	Anonymous function maker
X if Y else Z	Ternary selection (X is evaluated only if Y is true)
X or Y	Logical OR: Y is evaluated only if X is false
X and Y	Logical AND: Y is evaluated only if X is true
not X	Logical negation
X in Y, X not in Y	Membership: iterables, sets
X is Y, X is not Y	Object identity tests
X < Y, X <= Y, X > Y, X >= Y	Magnitude comparisons, set subset and superset
X == Y, X != Y	Equality operators
X | Y	Bitwise OR, set union
X ^ Y	Bitwise exclusive OR, set symmetric difference
X & Y	Bitwise AND, set intersection
X << Y, X >> Y	Shift X left, right by Y bits
X + Y, X – Y	Addition/concatenation, subtraction/set difference
X * Y, X % Y, X / Y, X // Y	Multiplication/repetition, remainder/format, division, floor division
-X, +X	Unary negation, identity
~X	Bitwise NOT complement (inversion)
X ** Y	Power (exponentiation)
X[i]	Indexing (sequence, mapping, others)
X[i:j:k]	Slicing (all bounds optional)
X(...)	Call (function, method, class, other callable)
X.attr	Attribute reference
(...)	Tuple, expression, generator expression
[...]	List, list comprehension

Operator	Description
{...}	Dictionary, set, dictionary and set comprehension

Operator Usage Notes

- In Python 2.6, value inequality can be written as either X != Y or X <> Y. In Python 3.0, the latter of these options is removed because it is redundant.

- In Python 2.6, a backquotes expression `X` works the same as repr(X), and converts objects to display strings. In Python 3.0, use the more readable str() and repr() built-in functions instead.

- In both Python 3.0 and 2.6, the X // Y *floor division* expression always truncates fractional remainders, and returns an integer result for integers.

- The X / Y expression performs *true division* in 3.0 (always retaining remainders in a floating-point result), and *classic division* in 2.6 (truncating remainders for integers).

- The syntax [...] is used for both list literals and list comprehension expressions. The latter of these performs an implied loop and collects expression results in a new list.

- The syntax (...) is used for tuples and expressions, as well as generator expressions—a form of list comprehension that produces results on demand, instead of building a result list. Parenthesis may sometimes be omitted in all three constructs.

- The syntax {...} is used for dictionary literals. In Python 3.0, it is also used for set literals, and both dictionary and set comprehensions; use set() and looping statements in 2.6.

- The yield and ternary if/else selection expressions are available in Python 2.5 and later. The former returns send() arguments in generators; the latter is a shorthand for a multiline if statement. yield requires parentheses if not alone on the right side of an assignment statement.

- Comparison operators may be chained: X < Y < Z produces the same result as X < Y and Y < Z, but Y is evaluated only once in the chained form.

- The slice expression `X[I:J:K]` is equivalent to indexing with a slice object: `X[slice(I, J, K)]`.

- In Python 2.6, magnitude comparisons of mixed types are allowed—converting numbers to a common type, and ordering other mixed types according to the type name. In Python 3.0, nonnumeric mixed-type magnitude comparisons are not allowed, and raise exceptions; this includes sorts by proxy.

- Magnitude comparisons for dictionaries are also no longer supported in Python 3.0 (though equality tests are); comparing `sorted(dict.items())` is one possible replacement in 3.0.

- Call expressions allow for positional and keyword arguments, and arbitrarily large numbers of both; see "The Expression Statement" on page 59 and "The def Statement" on page 64 for call syntax.

- Python 3.0 allows ellipsis (literally, `...`) to be used as an atomic expression anywhere in source code. This may be used as an alternative to `pass` or `None` in some contexts (e.g., stubbed-out function bodies, type-independent variable initialization).

Operations by Category

All built-in types support the comparisons and Boolean operations listed in Table 2.

Boolean `true` means any nonzero number or any nonempty collection object (list, dictionary, etc.). The built-in names `True` and `False` are pre-assigned to true and false values and behave like integers 1 and 0 with custom display formats. The special object `None` is false.

Comparisons return True or False and are applied recursively in compound objects as needed to determine a result.

Boolean and and or operators stop (short-circuit) as soon as a result is known and return one of the two operand objects (on left or right).

Table 2. Comparisons and Boolean operations

Operator	Description
X < Y	Strictly less than[a]
X <= Y	Less than or equal to
X > Y	Strictly greater than
X >= Y	Greater than or equal to
X == Y	Equal to (same value)
X != Y	Not equal to (same as X<>Y in Python 2.6 only)[b]
X is Y	Same object
X is not Y	Negated object identity
X < Y < Z	Chained comparisons
not X	If X is false then True; else, False
X or Y	If X is false then Y; else, X
X and Y	If X is false then X; else, Y

[a] To implement comparison expressions, see both the rich comparison (e.g., __lt__ for <) class methods in 3.0 and 2.6, and general __cmp__ method in 2.6, described in the section "Operator Overloading Methods" on page 88.

[b] != and <> both mean not equal by value in 2.6, but != is the preferred syntax in 2.6, and the only supported option in 3.0. is performs an identity test; == performs value comparison, and so is much more generally useful.

Tables 3 through 6 define operations common to types in the three major type categories (sequence, mapping, and number), as well as operations available for mutable (changeable) types in Python. Most types also export additional type-specific operations (e.g., methods), as described in the section "Specific Built-in Types" on page 16.

Table 3. Sequence operations (strings, lists, tuples, bytes, bytearray)

Operation	Description	Class method
X in S	Membership tests	__contains__,
X not in S		__iter__,
		__getitem__ [a]
S1 + S2	Concatenation	__add__
S * N, N * S	Repetition	__mul__
S[i]	Index by offset	__getitem__
S[i:j], S[i:j:k]	Slicing: items in S from offset i through j-1 by optional stride k	__getitem__ [b]
len(S)	Length	__len__
min(S), max(S)	Minimum, maximum item	__iter__,
		__getitem__
iter(S)	Iteration protocol	__iter__
for X in S:,	Iteration (all contexts)	__iter__,
[expr for X in S],		__getitem__
map(func, S), etc.		

[a] See also iterators, generators, and the __iter__ class method (see the section "The yield Statement" on page 68). If defined, __contains__ is preferred over __iter__, and __iter__ is preferred over __getitem__.

[b] In Python 2.6, you may also define __getslice__, __setslice__, and __delslice__ to handle slicing operations. In 3.0, these are removed in favor of passing slice objects to their item-based indexing counterparts. Slice objects may be used explicitly in indexing expressions in place of i:j:k bounds.

Table 4. Mutable sequence operations (lists, bytearray)

Operation	Description	Class method
S[i] = X	Index assignment: change item at existing offset i	__setitem__
S[i:j] = S2,	Slice assignment: S from i to j is replaced by S2, with optional stride k	__setitem__
S[i:j:k] = S2		
del S[i]	Index deletion	__delitem__

Operation	Description	Class method
del S[i:j], del S[i:j:k]	Slice deletion	__delitem__

Table 5. Mapping operations (dictionaries)

Operation	Description	Class method
D[k]	Index by key	__getitem__
D[k] = X	Key assignment: change or create entry for key k	__setitem__
del D[k]	Delete item by key	__delitem__
len(D)	Length (number of keys)	__len__
k in D	Key membership test[a]	Same as in Table 3
k not in D	Converse of k in D	Same as in Table 3
iter(S)	Iterator object for keys	Same as in Table 3
for k in D:, etc.	Iterate through keys in D (all iteration contexts)	Same as in Table 3

[a] In Python 2.X, key membership may also be coded as D.has_key(K). This method is removed in Python 3.0 in favor of the in expression, which is also generally preferred in 2.6. See "Dictionaries" on page 41.

Table 6. Numeric operations (all number types)

Operation	Description	Class method
X + Y, X – Y	Add, subtract	__add__, __sub__
X * Y, X / Y, X // Y, X % Y	Multiply, divide, floor divide, remainder	__mul__, __truediv__, __floordiv__, __mod__
-X, +X	Negative, identity	__neg__, __pos__
X | Y, X & Y, X ^ Y	Bitwise OR, AND, exclusive OR (integers)	__or__, __and__, __xor__

Operation	Description	Class method
X << N, X >> N	Bitwise left-shift, right-shift (integers)	__lshift__, __rshift__
~X	Bitwise invert (integers)	__invert__
X ** Y	X to the power Y	__pow__
abs(X)	Absolute value	__abs__
int(X)	Convert to integer[a]	__int__
float(X)	Convert to float	__float__
complex(X), complex(re,im)	Make a complex value	__complex__
divmod(X, Y)	Tuple: (X/Y, X%Y)	__divmod__
pow(X, Y [,Z])	Raise to a power	__pow__

[a] In Python 2.6, the long() built-in function invokes the __long__ class method. In Python 3.0, the int type subsumes long, which is removed.

Sequence Operation Notes

Indexing: S[i]

- Fetches components at offsets (first item is at offset 0).
- Negative indexes mean to count backward from the end (last item is at offset –1).
- S[0] fetches the first item.
- S[-2] fetches the second-to-last item (S[len(S) - 2]).

Slicing: S[i:j]

- Extracts contiguous sections of a sequence.
- Slice boundaries default to 0 and sequence length.
- S[1:3] fetches from offsets 1 up to, but not including, 3.
- S[1:] fetches from offsets 1 through the end (length-1).

- S[:-1] fetches from offsets 0 up to, but not including, the last item.
- S[:] makes a top-level (shallow) copy of sequence object S.
- Slice assignment is similar to deleting and then inserting.

Slicing: S[i:j:k]

- If present, the third item k is a stride: added to the offset of each item extracted.
- S[::2] is every other item in sequence S.
- S[::-1] is sequence S reversed.
- S[4:1:-1] fetches from offsets 4 up to, but not including, 1, reversed.

Other

- Concatenation, repetition, and slicing return new objects (not always for tuples).

Specific Built-in Types

This section covers numbers, strings, lists, dictionaries, tuples, files, and other core built-in types. Compound datatypes (e.g., lists, dictionaries, and tuples) can nest inside each other arbitrarily and as deeply as required. Sets may participate in nesting as well, but may contain only immutable objects.

Numbers

This section covers basic number types (integers, floating-point), as well as more advanced types (complex, decimals, and fractions). Numbers are always immutable (unchangeable).

Literals and creation

Numbers are written in a variety of numeric constant forms.

`1234, -24, 0`
> Integers (unlimited precision)[*]

`1.23, 3.14e-10, 4E210, 4.0e+210, 1., .1`
> Floating-point (normally implemented as C doubles in CPython)

`0o177, 0x9ff, 0b1111`
> Octal, hex, and binary literals for integers[†]

`3+4j, 3.0+4.0j, 3J`
> Complex numbers

`decimal.Decimal('1.33'), fractions.Fraction(4, 3)`
> Module-based types: decimal, fraction

`int(), float(), complex()`
> Create numbers from other objects, or from strings with possible base conversion; see "Built-in Functions" on page 102

Operations

Number types support all number operations (see Table 6 on page 14). In mixed-type expressions, Python converts operands up to the type of the "highest" type, where integer is lower than floating-point, which is lower than complex. As of Python 3.0 and 2.6, integer and floating-point objects also have a handful of *methods* and other *attributes*; see Python's Library Reference manual for details.

```
>>> (2.5).as_integer_ratio()          # float attributes
(5, 2)
```

---

[*] In Python 2.6, there is a distinct type named `long` for unlimited-precision integers; `int` is for normal integers with precision that is usually limited to 32 bits. Long objects may be coded with a trailing "L" (e.g., `99999L`), though integers are automatically promoted to longs if they require the extra precision. In 3.0, the `int` type provides unlimited precision and so subsumes both the 2.6 `int` and `long` types; the "L" literal syntax is removed in 3.0.

[†] In Python 2.6, octal literals may also be written with just a leading zero—`0777` and `0o777` are equivalent. In 3.0, only the latter form is supported for octal.

```
>>> (2.5).is_integer()
False

>>> (2).numerator, (2).denominator      # int attributes
(2, 1)
>>> (255).bit_length(), bin(255)        # 3.1+ bit_length()
(8, '0b11111111')
```

Decimal and fraction

Python provides two additional numeric types in standard library modules—*decimal* is a fixed-precision floating-point number, and *fraction* is a rational type that keeps numerator and denominator explicitly. Both may be used to address inaccuracies of floating-point arithmetic.

```
>>> 0.1 - 0.3
-0.19999999999999998

>>> from decimal import Decimal
>>> Decimal('0.1') - Decimal('0.3')
Decimal('-0.2')

>>> from fractions import Fraction
>>> Fraction(1, 10) - Fraction(3, 10)
Fraction(-1, 5)

>>> Fraction(1, 3) + Fraction(7, 6)
Fraction(3, 2)
```

Fractions automatically simplify results. By fixing precision and supporting various truncation and rounding protocols, decimals are useful for monetary applications. See the Python Library Reference for details.

Other numeric types

Python also includes a *set* type (described in "Sets" on page 49). Additional numeric types such as vectors and matrixes are available as third-party open source extensions (e.g., see the *NumPy* package). The third-party domain also includes support for visualization, statistical packages, and more.

Strings

The normal **str** string object is an immutable (i.e., unchangeable) array of characters, accessed by offset. As of Python 3.0, there are three string types with very similar interfaces:

- **str**, an immutable sequence of characters, used for all text, both ASCII and wider Unicode
- **bytes**, an immutable sequence of short integers, used for binary byte data
- **bytearray**, a mutable variant of bytes

Python 2.X instead has two immutable string types: **str**, for 8-bit text and binary data, and **unicode**, for Unicode text as described in "Unicode Strings" on page 33. Python 2.6 also has the Python 3.0 **bytearray** type as a back-port from 3.0, but it does not impose as sharp a distinction between text and binary data (it may be mixed with text strings freely in 2.6).

Most of this section pertains to all string types, but see "String methods" on page 26, "Unicode Strings" on page 33, and "Built-in Functions" on page 102 for more on **bytes** and **bytearray**.

Literals and creation

Strings are written as a series of characters in quotes, optionally preceded with a designator character.

`"Python's", 'Python"s'`
> Double and single quotes work the same, and each can embed unescaped quotes of the other kind.

`"""This is a multiline block"""`
> Triple-quoted blocks collect lines into a single string, with end-of-line markers (\n) inserted between the original lines.

`'Python\'s\n'`
> Backslash escape code sequences (see Table 7) are replaced with the special-character byte values they represent (e.g., '\n' is a byte with binary value **10** decimal).

```
"This" "is" "concatenated"
```
Adjacent string constants are concatenated. May span lines if parenthesized.

```
r'a raw\string', R'another\one'
```
Raw strings: backslashes are retained literally (except at the end of a string). Useful for regular expressions and DOS directory paths: e.g., `r'c:\dir1\file'`.

The following literal forms make specialized strings described in "Unicode Strings" on page 33:

```
b'...'
```
bytes string literal: sequence of 8-bit byte values representing raw binary data. Makes a **bytes** string in Python 3.0, and a normal **str** string in Python 2.6 (for 3.0 compatibility). See "String methods" on page 26, "Unicode Strings" on page 33, and "Built-in Functions" on page 102.

```
bytearray(...)
```
bytearray string construction: a mutable variant of **bytes**. Available in both Python 2.6 and 3.0. See "String methods" on page 26, "Unicode Strings" on page 33, and "Built-in Functions" on page 102.

```
u'...'
```
Unicode string literal in Python 2.X only (normal **str** strings support Unicode text in Python 3). See "Unicode Strings" on page 33.

```
str(), bytes(), bytearray()
```
Create strings from objects, with possible Unicode encoding/decoding in Python 3.0. See "Built-in Functions" on page 102.

```
hex(), oct(), bin()
```
Create hex/octal/binary digit strings from numbers. See "Built-in Functions" on page 102.

String literals may contain escape sequences taken from Table 7 to represent special bytes.

Table 7. String constant escape codes

Escape	Meaning	Escape	Meaning
\newline	Ignored continuation	\t	Horizontal tab
\\	Backslash (\)	\v	Vertical tab
\'	Single quote (')	\N{id}	Unicode dbase id
\"	Double quote (")	\uhhhh	Unicode 16-bit hex
\a	Bell	\Uhhhhhhhh	Unicode 32-bit hex[a]
\b	Backspace	\xhh	Hex (at most 2 digits)
\f	Formfeed	\ooo	Octal (up to 3 digits)
\n	Linefeed	\0	Null (not end of string)
\r	Carriage return	\other	Not an escape

[a] \Uhhhhhhhh takes exactly eight hexadecimal digits (h); both \u and \U can be used only in Unicode string literals.

Operations

All string types support all mutable sequence operations (shown earlier in Table 3 on page 13), plus string method calls (described ahead). In addition, the `str` type supports % string formatting expressions and template substitution, and the `bytearray` type supports mutable sequence operations (Table 4 on page 13, plus extra list-like methods). Also see the `re` string pattern-matching module in "The re Pattern-Matching Module" on page 155, and string-related built-in functions in the section "Built-in Functions" on page 102.

String formatting

In both Python 2.6 and 3.0, normal `str` strings support two different flavors of string formatting—operations that format objects according to format description strings:

* The original expression, coded with the % operator: `fmt % (values)`
* The new method, coded with call syntax: `fmt.format(values)`

Both produce new strings based on possibly type-specific substitution codes. Their results may be displayed or assigned to variables for later use:

```
>>> '%s, %s, %.2f' % (42, 'spam', 1 / 3.0)
'42, spam, 0.33'

>>> '{0}, {1}, {2:.2f}'.format(42, 'spam', 1 / 3.0)
'42, spam, 0.33'
```

Although the method call seems to be more actively evolving as these words are being written, the expression is used extensively in existing code, and both forms are still fully supported. Moreover, although some view the method form as marginally more mnemonic and consistent, the expression is often simpler and more concise. As these two forms are largely just minor variations on a theme of equivalent functionality and complexity, there is today no compelling reason to recommend one over the other.

String formatting expression

String formatting expressions replace % targets in the string on the left of the % operator, with values on the right (similar to C's sprintf). If more than one value is to be replaced, they must be coded as a tuple to the right of the % operator. If just one item is to be replaced, it can be coded as a single value or one-item tuple on the right (nest tuples to format a tuple itself). If key names are used on the left, a dictionary must be supplied on the right, and * allows width and precision to be passed in dynamically:

```
'The knights who say %s!' % 'Ni'
```
    Result: 'The knights who say Ni!'

```
"%d %s %d you" % (1, 'spam', 4.0)
```
    Result: '1 spam 4 you'

```
"%(n)d %(x)s" % {"n":1, "x":"spam"}
```
    Result: '1 spam'

```
'%f, %.2f, %.*f' % (1/3.0, 1/3.0, 4, 1/3.0)
```
    Result: '0.333333, 0.33, 0.3333'

In the format string on the left of the % operator, substitution targets have the following general format:

```
%[(keyname)][flags][width][.precision]typecode
```

keyname references an item in the expected dictionary; *flags* can be - (left-justify), + (numeric sign), a space (leave a blank before positive numbers), and 0 (zero fill); *width* is the total field width; *precision* gives digits after .; and *typecode* is a character from Table 8. Both *width* and *precision* can be coded as a * to force their values to be taken from the next item in the values to the right of the % operator when sizes are not known until runtime. Hint: %s converts any object to its print representation string.

Table 8. % string formatting type codes

Code	Meaning	Code	Meaning
s	String (or any object, uses str())	X	x with uppercase
r	s, but uses repr(), not str()	e	Floating-point exponent
c	Character (int or str)	E	e with uppercase
d	Decimal (base 10 integer)	f	Floating-point decimal
i	Integer	F	f with uppercase
u	Same as d (obsolete)	g	Floating-point e or f
o	Octal (base 8 integer)	G	Floating-point E or F
x	Hex (base 16 integer)	%	Literal '%'

String formatting method

The formatting method call works similar to the prior section's expression, but is invoked with normal method-call syntax on the format string object, and identifies substitution targets with {} syntax instead of %. Substitution targets in the format string may name method-call arguments by position or keyword name; may further reference argument attributes, keys, and offsets; may accept default formatting or provide explicit type codes; and may nest target syntax to pull values from the arguments list:

```
>>> '{0}, {food}'.format(42, food='spam')
'42, spam'

>>> import sys
>>> fmt = '{0.platform} {1[x]} {2[0]}'  # attr,key,index
>>> fmt.format(sys, {'x': 'ham', 'y': 'eggs'}, 'AB')
'win32 ham A'

>>> '{0} {1:+.2f}'.format(1 / 3.0, 1 / 3.0)
'0.333333333333 +0.33'

>>> '{0:.{1}f}'.format(1 / 3.0, 4)
'0.3333'
```

Most of these have equivalents in % expression usage patterns
(e.g., dictionary key and * value references), though the expression requires some operations to be coded outside the format string itself. Substitution targets in strings used for format
method calls take the following general form:

> {*fieldname*!*conversionflag*:*formatspec*}

In this substitution target syntax:

- **fieldname** is a number or keyword naming an argument,
  followed by optional ".name" attribute or "[index]" component references.
- **conversionflag** is "r", "s", or "a" to call repr(), str(), or
  ascii() on the value, respectively.
- **formatspec** specifies how the value should be presented,
  including details such as field width, alignment, padding,
  decimal precision, and so on, and ends with an optional
  data type code.

The **formatspec** component after the colon character is for-
mally described as follows (brackets in this denote optional
components and are not coded literally):

> [[*fill*]*align*][*sign*][#][0][*width*][.*precision*][*typecode*]

align may be "<", ">", "=", or "^", for left alignment, right alignments, padding after a sign character, or centered alignment, respectively. **sign** may be +, -, or space, and **typecode** is generally the same as that for % expressions in Table 8, with the following notable exceptions:

- The **i** and **u** type codes are absent; use **d** to display integers in decimal (base 10) format.

- An extra **b** type code displays integers in binary format (like using the **bin()** built-in).

- An extra **%** type code displays a number as a percentage.

A single object may also be formatted with the **format(*object*, *formatspec*)** built-in function (see "Built-in Functions" on page 102). Formatting may be customized with the **__format__** operator-overloading method in classes (see "Operator Overloading Methods" on page 88).

NOTE

In Python 3.1 and later, a "," preceding an integer or floating-point designation in **typecode** inserts thousands-separator commas:

```
'{0:,d}'.format(1000000)
```

creates '1,000,000', and:

```
'{0:13,.2f}'.format(1000000)
```

is ' 1,000,000.00'.

Also as of Python 3.1, field numbers are automatically numbered sequentially if omitted from **fieldname**—the following three have the same effect, though auto-numbered fields may be less readable if many fields are present:

```
'{0}/{1}/{2}'.format(x, y, z)  # explicit num
'{}/{}/{}'.format(x, y, z)     # 3.1 auto-num
'%s/%s/%s' % (x, y, z)         # expression
```

Template string substitution

In Python 2.4 and later, another form of simple string substitution is provided as an alternative to the string formatting expression and method described in the prior sections. The usual way of substituting variables is with the % operator:

```
>>> '%(page)i: %(title)s' % {'page':2, 'title': 'PyRef4E'}
'2: PyRef4E'
```

For simpler formatting tasks, a `Template` class has been added to the `string` module that uses `$` to indicate a substitution:

```
>>> import string
>>> t = string.Template('$page: $title')
>>> t.substitute({'page':2, 'title': 'PyRef4E'})
'2: PyRef4E'
```

Substitution values can be provided as keyword arguments or dictionary keys:

```
>>> s = string.Template('$who likes $what')
>>> s.substitute(who='bob', what=3.14)
'bob likes 3.14'
>>> s.substitute(dict(who='bob', what='pie'))
'bob likes pie'
```

A `safe_substitute` method ignores missing keys rather than raising an exception:

```
>>> t = string.Template('$page: $title')
>>> t.safe_substitute({'page':3})
'3: $title'
```

String methods

In addition to the `format()` method described earlier, string method calls provide higher-level text processing tools beyond string expressions. Table 9 lists available string method calls; `S` is any string object in this table. String methods that modify text always return a new string and never modify the object in-place (strings are immutable). See also the `re` module in the section "The re Pattern-Matching Module" on page 155 for pattern-based equivalents to some string type methods.

Table 9. Python 3.0 string method calls

```
S.capitalize()
S.center(width, [, fill])
S.count(sub [, start [, end]])
S.encode([encoding [,errors]])
S.endswith(suffix [, start [, end]])
S.expandtabs([tabsize])
S.find(sub [, start [, end]])
S.format(fmtstr, *args, **kwargs)
S.index(sub [, start [, end]])
S.isalnum()
S.isalpha()
S.isdecimal()
S.isdigit()
S.isidentifier()
S.islower()
S.isnumeric()
S.isprintable()
S.isspace()
S.istitle()
S.isupper()
S.join(iterable)
S.ljust(width [, fill])
S.lower()
S.lstrip([chars])
S.maketrans(x[, y[, z]])
S.partition(sep)
S.replace(old, new [, count])
S.rfind(sub [,start [,end]])
S.rindex(sub [, start [, end]])
```

```
S.rjust(width [, fill])
S.rpartition(sep)
S.rsplit([sep[, maxsplit]])
S.rstrip([chars])
S.split([sep [,maxsplit]])
S.splitlines([keepends])
S.startswith(prefix [, start [, end]])
S.strip([chars])
S.swapcase()
S.title()
S.translate(map)
S.upper()
S.zfill(width)
```

byte and bytearray methods

Python 3.0 bytes and bytearray string types have similar method sets, but do not overlap exactly with the normal str string type (str is Unicode text, bytes is raw binary data, and bytearray is mutable). In the following, set(X) - set(Y) computes items in X that are not in Y:

- bytes and bytearray do not support Unicode encoding (they are raw bytes, not decoded text) or string formatting (str.format and the % operator implemented with __mod__)

- str does not support Unicode decoding (it is already-decoded text)

- bytearray has unique mutable in-place methods similar to list:

  ```
  >>> set(dir(str)) - set(dir(bytes))
  {'isprintable', 'format', '__mod__', 'encode',
  'isidentifier', '_formatter_field_name_split',
  'isnumeric', '__rmod__', 'isdecimal',
  '_formatter_parser', 'maketrans'}
  ```

```
>>> set(dir(bytes)) - set(dir(str))
{'decode', 'fromhex'}

>>> set(dir(bytearray)) - set(dir(bytes))
{'insert', '__alloc__', 'reverse', 'extend',
'__delitem__', 'pop', '__setitem__',
'__iadd__', 'remove', 'append', '__imul__'}
```

Besides methods, **bytes** and **bytearray** also support the usual sequence operations in Table 3 on page 13, and **bytearray** supports mutable sequence operations in Table 4 on page 13. See more in "Unicode Strings" on page 33 and "Built-in Functions" on page 102.

NOTE

The set of string methods available in Python 2.6 varies slightly (e.g., there is a **decode** method for 2.6's different Unicode type model). The Python 2.6 **unicode** string type has a nearly identical interface to 2.6 **str** objects. Consult the Python 2.6 Library Reference or run **dir(str)** and **help(str.*method*)** interactively for more details.

The following sections go into more detail on some of the methods listed in Table 9. In all of the following that return a string result, the result is a new string. (Because strings are immutable, they are never modified in-place.) Whitespace means spaces, tabs, and end-of-line characters (everything in **string.whitespace**).

Searching

s.find(sub, [, start [, end]])
> Returns offset of the first occurrence of string **sub** in **s**, between offsets **start** and **end** (which default to **0** and **len(s)**, the entire string). Returns -1 if not found. Also see the **in** membership operator, which may be used to test substring membership in a string.

`s.rfind(sub, [, start [, end]])`

> Like `find`, but scans from the end (right to left).

`s.index(sub [, start [, end]])`

> Like `find`, but raises `ValueError` if not found instead of returning `-1`.

`s.rindex(sub [, start [, end]])`

> Like `rfind`, but raises `ValueError` if not found instead of returning `-1`.

`s.count(sub [, start [, end]])`

> Counts the number of nonoverlapping occurrences of `sub` in `s`, from offsets `start` to `end` (defaults: `0`, `len(s)`).

`s.startswith(sub [, start [, end]])`

> `True` if string `s` starts with substring `sub`. `start` and `end` give optional begin and end points for matching `sub`.

`s.endswith(sub [, start [, end]])`

> `True` if string `s` ends with substring `sub`. `start` and `end` give optional begin and end points for matching `sub`.

Splitting and joining

`s.split([sep [, maxsplit]])`

> Returns a list of the words in the string `s`, using `sep` as the delimiter string. If `maxsplit` is given, at most `maxsplit` splits are done. If `sep` is not specified or is `None`, any whitespace string is a separator. `'a*b'.split('*')` yields `['a','b']`. Use `list(s)` to convert a string to a list of characters (e.g., `['a','*','b']`).

`sep.join(iterable)`

> Concatenates an iterable (e.g., list or tuple) of strings into a single string, with `sep` added between each item. `sep` can be `''` (an empty string) to convert a list of characters to a string (`'*'.join(['a','b'])` yields `'a*b'`).

`s.replace(old, new [, count])`

> Returns a copy of string `s` with all occurrences of substring `old` replaced by `new`. If `count` is passed, the first `count` occurrences are replaced. This works like a combination of `x=s.split(old)` and `new.join(x)`.

`s.splitlines([keepends])`

    Splits string `s` on line breaks, returning lines list. The result does not retain line break characters unless `keepends` is true.

Formatting

`s.capitalize()`

    Capitalizes the first character of string `s`.

`s.expandtabs([tabsize])`

    Replaces tabs in string `s` with `tabsize` spaces (default is 8).

`s.strip([chars])`

    Removes leading and trailing whitespace from string `s` (or characters in `chars` if passed).

`s.lstrip([chars])`

    Removes leading whitespace from string `s` (or characters in `chars` if passed).

`s.rstrip([chars])`

    Removes trailing whitespace from string `s` (or characters in `chars` if passed).

`s.swapcase()`

    Converts all lowercase letters to uppercase, and vice versa.

`s.upper()`

    Converts all letters to uppercase.

`s.lower()`

    Converts all letters to lowercase.

`s.ljust(width [, fill])`

    Left-justifies string `s` in a field of the given `width`; pads on right with character `fill` (which defaults to a space). The String formatting expression and method can achieve similar effects.

`s.rjust(width [, fill])`

    Right-justifies string `s` in a field of the given `width`; pads on left with character `fill` (which defaults to a space). The String formatting expression and method can achieve similar effects.

```
s.center(width [, fill])
```
Centers string s in a field of the given width; pads on left and right with character fill (which defaults to a space). The String formatting expression and method can achieve similar effects.

```
s.zfill(width)
```
Pads string s on left with zero digits to produce a string result of the desired width (can also achieve with % string formatting expression).

```
s.translate(table [, deletechars])
```
Deletes all characters from string s that are in deletechars (if present), then translates the characters using table, a 256-character string giving the translation for each character value indexed by its ordinal.

```
s.title()
```
Returns a title-cased version of the string: words start with uppercase characters; all remaining cased characters are lowercase.

Content tests

```
s.is*()
```
The is*() Boolean tests work on strings of any length. They test the content of strings for various categories (and always return False for an empty).

The original string module

Starting in Python 2.0, most of the string-processing functions previously available in the standard string module became available as methods of string objects. If X references a string object, a string module function call such as:

```
import string
res = string.replace(X, 'span', 'spam')
```

is usually equivalent in Python 2.0 to a string method call such as:

```
res = X.replace('span', 'spam')
```

But the string method call form is preferred and quicker, and string methods require no module imports. Note that the `string.join(list, delim)` operation becomes a method of the delimiter string `delim.join(list)`. All these functions are removed from the `string` module in Python 3.0: use the equivalent string object methods instead.

Unicode Strings

Technically, all text is Unicode text, including the simple 8-bit ASCII encoding scheme. Python supports Unicode (wide) character strings, which represent each character with 16 or more bits, not 8. This support differs in Python lines. Python 3.0 treats all text as Unicode and represents binary data separately, while Python 2.X distinguishes 8-bit text (and data) from wider Unicode text. Specifically:

- In *Python 2.6*, the `str` type represents both 8-bit text and binary data, and a separate `unicode` type handles wide-character Unicode text. A `u'ccc'` literal form supports coding binary data, and a `codecs` module supports reading and writing files containing Unicode text.

- In *Python 3.0*, the normal `str` string type and literal handles all text (both 8 bit and wider Unicode), and a separate `bytes` type represents 8-bit binary data. `bytes` may be coded with the `b'ccc'` literal form; it is an immutable sequence of small integers, but supports most `str` operations, and prints as ASCII text when possible. Also in 3.0, files imply `str` and `bytes` objects in text and binary mode; text mode files automatically encode and decode text; and an additional `bytearray` type is a mutable variant of `bytes`, with extra list-like methods for in-place changes. `bytearray` is also present in 2.6, but `bytes` is not (`b'ccc'` creates a `str` in 2.6 for compatibility).

Unicode support in Python 3.0

Python 3.0 allows non-ASCII characters to be coded in strings with hex (\x) and both 16- and 32-bit Unicode (\u, \U) escapes. In addition, `chr()` supports Unicode character codes:

```
>>> 'A\xE4B'
'AäB'
>>> 'A\u00E4B'
'AäB'
>>> 'A\U000000E4B'
'AäB'
>>> chr(0xe4)
'ä'
```

Normal strings may be encoded into raw bytes and raw bytes may be decoded into normal strings, using either default or explicit encodings:

```
>>> 'A\xE4B'.encode('latin-1')
b'A\xe4B'
>>> 'A\xE4B'.encode()
b'A\xc3\xa4B'
>>> 'A\xE4B'.encode('utf-8')
b'A\xc3\xa4B'
>>>
>>> b'A\xC3\xA4B'.decode('utf-8')
'AäB'
```

File objects also automatically decode and encode on input and output, and accept an encoding name to override the default encoding:

```
>>> S = 'A\xE4B'
>>> open('uni.txt', 'w', encoding='utf-8').write(S)
3
>>> open('uni.txt', 'rb').read()
b'A\xc3\xa4B'
>>>
>>> open('uni.txt', 'r', encoding='utf-8').read()
'AäB'
```

byte and bytearray strings

Python 3.0 `bytes` and `bytearray` string objects represent 8-bit binary data (including encoded Unicode text); print in ASCII

Operations

Operations include all sequence operations (see Table 3 on page 13), plus all mutable sequence operations (see Table 4 on page 13), plus the following list methods:

`alist.append(x)`

Inserts the single object x at the end of `alist`, changing the list in-place.

`alist.extend(x)`

Inserts each item in any iterable x at the end of `alist` in-place (an in-place +). Similar to `alist[len(alist):]` = `list(x)`.

`alist.sort(key=None, reverse=False)`

Sorts `alist` in-place, in ascending order by default. If passed, `key` specifies a function of one argument that is used to extract or compute a comparison value from each list element. If `reverse` is passed and `true`, the list elements are sorted as if each comparison were reversed. For example: `alist.sort(key=str.lower, reverse=True)`. See also the `sorted()` built-in function.

`alist.reverse()`

Reverses items in `alist` in-place.

`alist.index(x [, i [, j]])`

Returns the index of the first occurrence of object x in `alist`; raises an exception if not found. This is a search method. If `i` and `j` are passed, it returns the smallest k such that `s[k]` == x and `i` <= k < `j`.

`alist.insert(i, x)`

Inserts object x into `alist` at offset i (like `alist[i:i]` = `[x]`, for positive i).

`alist.count(x)`

Returns the number of occurrences of x in `alist`.

`alist.remove(x)`

Deletes the first occurrence of object x from `alist`; raises an exception if not found. Same as `del alist[alist.index(x)]`.

```
alist.pop([i])
```
> Deletes and returns the last (or offset `i`) item in `alist`. Use with `append` to implement stacks. Same as `x=alist[i];` `del alist[i]; return x`, where `i` defaults to `-1`, the last item.

NOTE

In Python 2.X, the list `sort` method signature is `alist.sort(cmp=None, key=None, reverse=False)`, where `cmp` is a two-argument comparison function, which returns a value less than, equal to, or greater than zero to denote a less, equal, and greater result. The comparison function is removed in 3.0 because it was typically used to map sort values and reverse sort order—use cases supported by the remaining two arguments.

List comprehension expressions

A list literal enclosed in square brackets (`[ ... ]`) can be a simple list of expressions or a list comprehension expression of the following form:

```
[expression for expr1 in iterable1 [if condition1]
            for expr2 in iterable2 [if condition2] ...
            for exprN in iterableN [if conditionN] ]
```

List comprehensions construct result lists: they collect all values of *expression*, for each iteration of all nested **for** loops, for which each optional *condition* is true. The second through *n*th **for** loops and all **if** parts are optional, and *expression* and *condition* can use variables assigned by nested **for** loops. Names bound inside the comprehension are created in the scope where the comprehension resides in 2.X (but local to the expression in 3.X).

Comprehensions are similar to the `map()` built-in function:

```
>>> [ord(x) for x in 'spam']
[115, 112, 97, 109]
>>> map(ord, 'spam')
[115, 112, 97, 109]
```

but can often avoid creating a temporary helper function:

```
>>> [x**2 for x in range(5)]
[0, 1, 4, 9, 16]
>>> map((lambda x: x**2), range(5))
[0, 1, 4, 9, 16]
```

Comprehensions with conditions are similar to `filter`:

```
>>> [x for x in range(5) if x % 2 == 0]
[0, 2, 4]
>>> filter((lambda x: x % 2 == 0), range(5))
[0, 2, 4]
```

Comprehensions with nested `for` loops are similar to the normal `for`:

```
>>> [y for x in range(3) for y in range(3)]
[0, 1, 2, 0, 1, 2, 0, 1, 2]

>>> res = []
>>> for x in range(3):
...     for y in range(3):
...         res.append(y)
>>> res
[0, 1, 2, 0, 1, 2, 0, 1, 2]
```

Generator expressions

As of Python 2.4, generator expressions achieve results similar to list comprehensions, without generating a physical list to hold all results. Generator expressions define a set of results, but do not materialize the entire list, to save memory; instead, they create a generator that will return elements one by one in iteration contexts. For example:

```
ords = (ord(x) for x in aString if x not in skipThese)
for o in ords:
    ...
```

Generator expressions are written inside parentheses rather than square brackets, but otherwise support all list comprehension syntax. The parentheses used for a function with a single argument suffice when creating an iterator to be passed to a function:

```
sum(ord(x) for x in aString)
```

Generator expression loop variables (x, in the prior example) are not accessible outside the generator expression. In Python 2.X, list comprehensions leave the variable assigned to its last value; Python 3.0 changes this to make list comprehensions' scope work like generator expressions.

Use the iterator protocol's __next__() method (next() in Python 2.X) to step through results outside iteration contexts such as for loops, and use the list call to produce a list of all results, if required:

```
>>> squares = (x ** 2 for x in range(5))
>>> squares
<generator object <genexpr> at 0x027C1AF8>
>>> squares.__next__()
0
>>> squares.__next__()                   # or next(squares)
1
>>> list(x ** 2 for x in range(5))
[0, 1, 4, 9, 16]
```

See "The yield Statement" on page 68 for more on generators and iterators, including additional generator methods.

Other generators and comprehensions

See also the related yield statement, dictionary comprehensions, and set comprehensions elsewhere in this book. The latter two are similar expressions that produce dictionaries and sets; they support syntax identical to list comprehensions and generator expressions, but are coded within {}, and dictionary comprehensions begin with a key:value expression pair:

```
>>> [x * x for x in range(10)]      # List comp.
[0, 1, 4, 9, 16, 25, 36, 49, 64, 81]

>>> (x * x for x in range(10))      # Generator expr.
<generator object at 0x009E7328>

>>> {x * x for x in range(10)}      # Set comp. (3.0)
{0, 1, 4, 81, 64, 9, 16, 49, 25, 36}

>>> {x: x * x for x in range(10)}   # Dict comp. (3.0)
{0: 0, 1: 1, 2: 4, 3: 9, 4: 16, 5: 25, 6: 36, 7: 49,
 8: 64, 9: 81}
```

Dictionaries

Dictionaries are mutable tables of object references, accessed by key, not position. They are unordered collections, implemented internally as dynamically expandable hash tables. Dictionaries have changed significantly in Python 3.0:

- In Python 2.X, the `keys()`/`values()`/`items()` methods return lists; there is a `has_key()` lookup method; there are distinct iterator methods `iterkeys()`/`itervalues()`/`iteritems()`; and dictionaries may be compared directly.

- In Python 3.0, the `keys()`/`values()`/`items()` methods return iterable *view* objects instead of lists; `has_key()` is removed in favor of `in` expressions; Python 2.X iterator methods are removed in favor of view object iteration; dictionaries cannot be compared directly, but their `sorted(D.items())` can; and there is a new dictionary comprehension expression.

- Python 3.0 *view* objects produce results on demand, retain the original order in the dictionary, reflect future dictionary changes, and may support set operations. Key views are always set-like, value views never are, and item views are if all their items are unique and hashable (immutable). See "Sets" on page 49 for set expressions that may be applied to some views. Pass views to the `list()` call to force generation of all their results at once (e.g., for display, or for `list.sort()`).

Literals and creation

Dictionary literals are written as comma-separated series of *key:value* pairs inside curly braces, the `dict()` built-in supports other creation patterns, and comprehensions employ iteration in Python 3.0. Assigning to new keys generates new entries. Any immutable object can be a key (e.g., string, number, tuple), and class instances can be keys if they inherit hashing protocol methods. Tuple keys support compound values (e.g., `adict[(M,D,Y)]`, with parentheses optional).

`{}`
> An empty dictionary.

`{'spam': 2, 'eggs': 3}`
> A two-item dictionary: keys `'spam'` and `'eggs'`.

`adict = { 'info': { 42: 1, type("): 2 }, 'spam': [] }`
> Nested dictionaries: `adict['info'][42]` fetches `1`.

`adict = dict(name='Bob', age=45, job=('mgr', 'dev'))`
> Creates a dictionary by passing keyword arguments to the type constructor.

`adict = dict(zip('abc', [1, 2, 3]))`
> Creates a dictionary by passing key/value tuples list to the type constructor.

`adict = dict([['a', 1], ['b', 2], ['c', 3]])`
> Same effect as prior line: any iterable of keys and values.

`adict = {c: ord(c) for c in 'spam'}`
> Dictionary comprehension expression (Python 3). See "List comprehension expressions" on page 38 for syntax.

Operations

Operations comprise all mapping operations (see Table 5 on page 14), plus the following dictionary-specific methods.

`adict.keys()`
> All keys in `adict`. In Python 2.X, this returns a list. In Python 3.0, it returns an iterable view object described earlier. `for k in adict:` also supports keys iteration.

`adict.values()`
> All stored values in `adict`. In Python 2.X, this returns a list. In Python 3.0, it returns an iterable view object described earlier.

`adict.items()`
> Tuple pairs `(key, value)`, one for each entry in `adict`. In Python 2.X, this returns a list. In Python 3.0, it returns an iterable view object described earlier.

```
adict.clear()
```
Removes all items from `adict`.

```
adict.copy()
```
Returns a shallow (top-level) copy of `adict`.

```
dict1.update(dict2)
```
Merges all of `dict2`'s entries into `dict1`, in-place, similar to `for (k, v) in dict2.items(): dict1[k] = v`. In Python 2.4, also accepts an iterable of key/value pairs, as well as keyword arguments (`dict.update(k1=v1, k2=v2)`).

```
adict.get(key [, default])
```
Similar to `adict[key]`, but returns `default` (or `None` if no `default`) instead of raising an exception when `key` is not found in `adict`.

```
adict.setdefault(key, [, default])
```
Same as `adict.get(key, default)`, but also assigns `key` to `default` if it is not found in `adict`.

```
adict.popitem()
```
Removes and returns an arbitrary (`key`, `value`) pair.

```
adict.pop(k [, default])
```
Returns `adict[k]` if `k in adict` (and removes `k`); else, returns `default`.

```
dict.fromkeys(seq [, value])
```
Creates a new dictionary with keys from `seq` and values set to `value` (callable on instance or type name).

The following methods are available in Python 2.X only:

```
adict.has_key(k)
```
Returns `True` if `adict` has a key `k`, or `False` otherwise. In Python 2.X only, this method is equivalent to `k in adict`, but is not generally recommended; it is removed in Python 3.0.

```
adict.iteritems(), adict.iterkeys(), adict.itervalues()
```
Returns an iterator over key/value pairs, keys only, or values only. In Python 3.0, these are removed because `keys()`, `values()`, and `items()` return iterable view objects.

The following operations are described in Table 5 on page 14, but relate to methods above:

`k in adict`

> Returns `True` if `adict` has a key `k`, or `False` otherwise. Replaces `has_key()` in Python 3.0.

`for k in adict:`

> Iterates over keys in `adict` (all iteration contexts). Dictionary supports direct iteration. `for key in dict` is similar to `for key in dict.keys()`. The former uses the dictionary object's keys iterator. In Python 2.X, `keys()` returns a new list that incurs a slight overhead. In Python 3.0, `keys()` returns an iterable view object instead of a physically stored list, making both forms equivalent.

Tuples

Tuples are immutable arrays of object references, accessed by offset.

Literals

Tuples are written as comma-separated series of values enclosed in parentheses. The enclosing parentheses can sometimes be omitted (e.g., in **for** loop headers and = assignments).

`()`

> An empty tuple.

`(0,)`

> A one-item tuple (not a simple expression).

`(0, 1, 2, 3)`

> A four-item tuple.

`0, 1, 2, 3`

> Another four-item tuple (same as prior line); not valid in function calls.

`atuple = ('spam', (42, 'eggs'))`

> Nested tuples: `atuple[1][1]` fetches `'eggs'`.

```
atuple = tuple('spam')
```
> Creates a tuple of all items in any iterable, by calling the type constructor function.

Operations

All sequence operations (see Table 3 on page 13), plus the following tuple-specific methods in Python 2.6, 3.0, and later:

```
atuple.index(x [, i [, j]])
```
> Returns the index of the first occurrence of object x in atuple; raises an exception if not found. This is a search method. If i and j are passed, it returns the smallest k such that s[k] == x and i <= k < j.

```
atuple.count(x)
```
> Returns the number of occurrences of x in atuple.

Files

The built-in open() function creates a file object, the most common file interface. File objects export the data transfer method calls in the next section. In Python 2.X only, the name file() can be used as a synonym for open() when creating a file object, but open() is the generally recommended spelling; in Python 3.0, file() is no longer available.

See the open() function in the section "Built-in Functions" on page 102 for full file-creation details. See also "Unicode Strings" on page 33 for the distinction between text and binary files and their corresponding implied string type differences in Python 3.0.

Related file-like tools covered later in this book: see the dbm, shelve, and pickle modules in the section "Object Persistence Modules" on page 163; the os module descriptor-based file functions and the os.path directory path tools in the section "The os System Module" on page 141; and the Python SQL database API in the section "Python Portable SQL Database API" on page 179.

Input files

```
infile = open('data.txt', 'r')
```
> Creates input file ('r' means read as text, while 'rb' reads binary with no line-break translation). The filename string (e.g., 'data.txt') maps to the current working directory, unless it includes a directory path prefix (e.g., 'c:\\dir\\data.txt'). The mode argument (e.g., 'r') is optional and defaults to 'r'.

```
infile.read()
```
> Reads entire file, returning its contents as a single string. In text mode ('r'), line-ends are translated to '\n' by default. In binary mode ('rb'), the result string can contain nonprintable characters (e.g., '\0'). In Python 3.0, text mode decodes Unicode text into a str string, and binary returns unaltered content in a bytes.

```
infile.read(N)
```
> Reads at most N more bytes (1 or more); empty at end-of-file.

```
infile.readline()
```
> Reads next line (through end-of-line marker); empty at end-of-file.

```
infile.readlines()
```
> Reads entire file into a list of line strings. See also file iterators, discussed next.

```
for line in infile:
```
> Uses file iterators to step through lines in a file automatically. Also available in all other iteration contexts (e.g., [line[:-1] for line in open('filename')]). The iteration for line in fileobj: has an effect similar to for line in fileobj.readlines():, but the file iterator version does not load the entire file into memory and so is more efficient.

Output files

```
outfile = open('/tmp/spam', 'w')
```
Creates output file. (Note that `'w'` means write text; `'wb'` writes binary data with no line-break translation.)

```
outfile.write(S)
```
Writes string S onto file (all bytes in S, with no formatting applied). In text mode, `'\n'` is translated to the platform-specific line-end marker sequence by default. In binary mode, the string can contain nonprintable bytes (e.g., use `'a\0b\0c'` to write a string of five bytes, two of which are binary zero). In Python 3.0, text mode encodes **str** Unicode strings, and binary mode writes **bytes** strings unaltered.

```
outfile.writelines(L)
```
Writes all strings in list L onto file.

Any files

```
file.close()
```
Manual close to free resources (Python currently auto-closes files if still open when they are garbage-collected). See also the upcoming file object context manager discussion.

```
file.tell()
```
Returns the file's current position.

```
file.seek(offset [, whence])
```
Sets the current file position to **offset** for random access. **whence** can be 0 (offset from front), 1 (offset +/– from current position), or 2 (offset from end). **whence** defaults to 0.

```
file.isatty()
```
Returns 1 if the file is connected to a tty-like interactive device.

```
file.flush()
```
Flushes the file's **stdio** buffer. Useful for buffered pipes, if another process (or human) is reading. Also useful for files created and read in the same process.

`file.truncate([size])`

> Truncates file to, at most, `size` bytes (or current position if no size is passed). Not available on all platforms.

`file.fileno()`

> Gets file number (descriptor integer) for file. This roughly converts file objects to descriptors that can be passed to tools in the `os` module. Use `os.fdopen` to convert a descriptor to a file object, `socketobj.makefile` to convert a socket to a file object, and `io.StringIO` (`StringIO.StringIO` in Python 2.X) to convert a string to an object with a file-like interface.

Attributes (all read-only)

`file.closed`

> `True` if file has been closed.

`file.mode`

> Mode string (e.g., `'r'`) passed to `open` function.

`file.name`

> String name of corresponding external file.

File context managers

In standard Python (CPython), file objects normally close themselves when garbage collected if still open. Because of this, temporary files (e.g., `open('name').read()`) need not be closed explicitly. To guarantee closes after a block of code exits, regardless of whether the block raises an exception, use the `try/finally` statement and manual closes:

```
myfile = open(r'C:\misc\script', 'w')
try:
    ...use myfile...
finally:
    myfile.close()
```

Or use the `with/as` statement available as of Python 2.6 and 3.0:

```
with open(r'C:\misc\script', 'w') as myfile:
    ...use myfile...
```

The first of these inserts a close call as a termination-time action. The latter of these employs file object context managers, which guarantee that a file is automatically closed when the enclosed code block exits. See the `try` and `with` statements in "Statements and Syntax" on page 53.

Notes

- Some file-open modes (e.g., `'r+'`) allow a file to be both input and output, and others (e.g., `'rb'`) specify binary-mode transfer to suppress line-end marker conversions (and Unicode encodings in Python 3.0). See `open()` in the section "Built-in Functions" on page 102.

- File-transfer operations occur at the current file position, but `seek` method calls reposition the file for random access.

- File transfers can be made *unbuffered*: see `open()` in the section "Built-in Functions" on page 102, and the `-u` command-line flag in the section "Command-Line Options" on page 4.

- Python 2.X also includes an `xreadlines()` file object method, which works the same as the file object's automatic line iterator, and has been removed in Python 3.0 due to its redundancy.

Sets

Sets are mutable and unordered collections of unique and immutable objects. Sets support mathematical set operations such as union and intersection. They are not sequences (they are unordered), and not mappings (they do not map values to keys), but support iteration, and function much like value-less (or keys-only) dictionaries.

Literals and creation

In Python 2.X and 3.0, sets may be created by calling the `set()` built-in function with an iterable whose items become members of the resulting set. In Python 3.0, sets may also be created by {...} set literal and set comprehension expression syntax, though `set()` is still used to make an empty set ({} is the empty dictionary), and to build sets from existing objects. Sets are mutable, but items in a set must be immutable; the `frozenset()` built-in creates an immutable set, which can be nested within another set.

```
set()
```
    An empty set

```
aset = set('spam')
```
    A four-item set: values `'s'`, `'p'`, `'a'`, `'m'` (accepts any iterable)

```
aset = {'s', 'p', 'a', 'm'}
```
    A four-item set, same as prior line (Python 3)

```
aset = {ord(c) for c in 'spam'}
```
    Sets comprehension expression (Python 3); see "List comprehension expressions" on page 38 for syntax

```
aset = frozenset(range(-5, 5))
```
    A frozen (immutable) set of 10 integers `-5...4`

Operations

The following documents the most prominent set operations but is not complete; see Python's Library Reference for an exhaustive list of set expressions and methods available. Most expression operators require two sets, but their method-based equivalents accept any iterable, denoted by "other" in the following (e.g., `{1, 2} | [2, 3]` fails, but `{1, 2}.union([2, 3])` works):

```
value in aset
```
    Membership: returns `True` if `aset` contains `value`

```
set1 - set2, set1.difference(other)
```
    Difference: new set containing items in `set1` that are not in `set2`

```
set1 | set2, set1.union(other)
```
    Union: new set containing items in either `set1` or `set2` with no duplicates

```
set1 & set2, set1.intersection(other)
```
    Intersection: new set containing items in both **set1** and **set2**

```
set1 <= set2, set1.issubset(other)
```
    Subset: tests whether every element in **set1** is also in **set2**

```
set1 >= set2, set1.issubset(other)
```
    Superset: tests whether every element in **set2** is also in **set1**

```
set1 < set2, set1 > set2
```
    True subset and superset: also tests that **set1** and **set2** are not the same

```
set1 ^ set2, set1.symmetric_difference(other)
```
    Symmetric difference: new set with elements in either **set1** or **set2** but not both

```
set1 |= set2, set1.update(other)
```
    Updates (not for frozen sets): adds items in **set2** to **set1**

```
set1.add(X), set1.remove(X), set1.discard(X), set1.pop(),
set1.clear()
```
    Updates (not for frozen sets): adds an item, removes an item, removes an item if present, removes and returns an arbitrary item, removes all items

```
len(aset)
```
    Length: numbers items in set

```
for x in aset:
```
    Iteration: all iteration contexts

```
aset.copy()
```
    Makes a copy of **aset**; same as **set(aset)**

Other Common Types

Python's core types also include *Booleans* (described next); **None** (a placeholder object); *types* (accessed with the **type()** built-in function, and always classes in Python 3); and *program-unit* types such as functions, modules, and classes (runtime object in Python).

Boolean

The Boolean type, named **bool**, provides two predefined constants, named **True** and **False** (available since version 2.3). For most purposes, these constants can be treated as though they were pre-assigned to integers 1 and 0, respectively (e.g., **True** + **3** yields **4**). However, the **bool** type is a subclass of the integer type **int**, and customizes it to print instances differently (**True** prints as "True", not "1", and may be used as a built-in name in logical tests).

Type Conversions

Tables 10 and 11 define common built-in tools for converting from one type to another. (Python 2 also supports a **long(S)** to-long and `X` to-string converters removed in Python 3.0.)

Table 10. Sequence converters

Converter	Converts from	Converts to
list(X), [n for n in X][a]	String, tuple, any iterable	List
tuple(X)	String, list, any iterable	Tuple
''.join(X)	Iterable of strings	String

[a] The list comprehension form may be slower than list(). In Python 2.X only, map(None, X) has the same effect as list(X) in this context, though this form of map is removed in Python 3.0.

Table 11. String/object converters

Converter	Converts from	Converts to
eval(S)	String	Any object with a syntax (expression)
int(S [, base]),[a] float(S)	String or number	Integer, float
repr(X), str(X)	Any Python object	String (repr is as code, str is user-friendly)

Converter	Converts from	Converts to
F % X, F.format(X)	Objects with format codes	String
hex(X), oct(X), bin(X), str(X)	Integer types	Hexadecimal, octal, binary, decimal digit strings
ord(C), chr(I)	Character, integer code	Integer code, character

[a] In version 2.2 and later, converter functions (e.g., int, float, str) also serve as class constructors and can be subclassed. In Python 3.0, all types are classes, and all classes are instances of the type class.

Statements and Syntax

This section describes the rules for syntax and variable names.

Syntax Rules

Here are the general rules for writing Python programs:

Control flow

Statements execute one after another, unless control-flow statements are used (if, while, for, raise, calls, etc.).

Blocks

A block is delimited by indenting all of its statements by the same amount, with spaces or tabs. A tab counts for enough spaces to move the column to a multiple of 8. Blocks can appear on the same line as a statement header if they are simple statements.

Statements

A statement ends at the end of a line, but can continue over multiple lines if a physical line ends with a \, an unclosed (), [], or {} pair, or an unclosed, triple-quoted string. Multiple simple statements can appear on a line if they are separated with a semicolon (;).

Comments

Comments start with a # (not in a string constant) and span to the end of the line.

Documentation strings

If a function, module file, or class begins with a string literal, it is stored in the object's `__doc__` attribute. See the `help()` function, and the `pydoc` module and script in the Python Library Reference for automated extraction and display tools.

Whitespace

Generally significant only to the left of code, where indentation is used to group blocks. Blank lines and spaces are otherwise ignored except as token separators and within string constants.

Name Rules

This section contains the rules for user-defined names (i.e., variables) in programs.

Name format

Structure

User-defined names start with a letter or underscore (_), followed by any number of letters, digits, or underscores.

Reserved words

User-defined names cannot be the same as any Python reserved word listed in Table 12.[‡]

Case sensitivity

User-defined names and reserved words are always case-sensitive: *SPAM*, *spam*, and *Spam* are different names.

Unused tokens

Python does not use the characters $ and ? in its syntax, though they can appear in string constants and comments, and $ is special in string template substitution.

---

‡ In the Jython Java-based implementation, user-defined names can sometimes be the same as reserved words.

Creation

User-defined names are created by assignment but must exist when referenced (e.g., counters must be explicitly initialized to zero). See the section "Namespace and Scope Rules" on page 82.

Table 12. Python 3.0 reserved words

False	class	finally	is	return
None	continue	for	lambda	try
True	def	from	nonlocal	while
and	del	global	not	with
as	elif	if	or	yield
assert	else	import	pass	
break	except	in	raise	

NOTE

In Python 2.6, print and exec are both reserved words, as they take the form of statements, not built-in functions. Also in Python 2.6, nonlocal, True, and False are not reserved words; the first of these is unavailable, and the latter two are simply built-in names. with and as are reserved in both 2.6 and 3.0, but not in earlier 2.X releases unless context managers are explicitly enabled. yield is reserved as of 2.3; it morphed from statement to expression later but is still a reserved word.

Name conventions

- Names that begin and end with two underscores (for example, __init__) have a special meaning to the interpreter but are not reserved words.

- Names beginning with one underscore (e.g., _X) and assigned at the top level of a module are not copied out by from...* imports (see also the __all__ module export names list, mentioned in the sections "The from Statement" on page 72 and

"Pseudoprivate Attributes" on page 86). In other contexts, this is an informal convention for internal names.

- Names beginning but not ending with two underscores (e.g., __X) within a **class** statement are prefixed with the enclosing class's name (see "Pseudoprivate Attributes" on page 86).

- The name that is just a single underscore (_) is used in the interactive interpreter (only) to store the result of the last evaluation.

- Built-in function and exception names (e.g., open, SyntaxError) are not reserved words. They live in the last-searched scope and can be reassigned to hide the built-in meaning in the current scope (e.g., open=myfunction).

- Class names commonly begin with an uppercase letter (e.g., MyClass), and modules with a lowercase letter (e.g., mymodule).

- The first (leftmost) argument in a class method function is usually named self.

Specific Statements

The following sections describe all Python statements. Each section lists the statement's syntax formats, followed by usage details. For compound statements, each appearance of a *suite* in a statement format stands for one or more other statements, possibly indented as a block under a header line. A suite must be indented under a header if it contains another compound statement (**if**, **while**, etc.); otherwise, it can appear on the same line as the statement header. The following are both valid constructs:

```
if x < 42:
    print(x)
    while x: x = x - 1

if x < 42: print(x)
```

The Assignment Statement

```
target = expression
target1 = target2 = expression
target1, target2 = expression1, expression2
target1 += expression
target1, target2, ...  = same-length-iterable
(target1, target2, ...) = same-length-iterable
[target1, target2, ...] = same-length-iterable
target1, *target2, ...  = matching-length-iterable
```

Assignments store references to objects in targets. Expressions yield objects. Targets can be simple names (X), qualified attributes (X.attr), or indexes and slices (X[i], X[i:j]).

The second format assigns an *expression* object to each target. The third format pairs targets with expressions, left to right. The last three formats assign components of any sequence (or other iterable) to corresponding targets, from left to right. The sequence or iterable on the right must be the same length but can be any type, unless a single starred-name appears in the targets on the left to collect arbitrarily many items (Python 3.0 extended sequence assignment, discussed ahead):

```
target1, *target2, ... = iterable
```

Augmented assignment

A set of additional assignment statement formats, listed in Table 13, are available. Known as *augmented assignments*, these formats imply a binary expression plus an assignment. For instance, the following two formats are roughly equivalent:

```
X = X + Y
X += Y
```

However, the reference to target X in the second format needs to be evaluated only once, and in-place operations can be applied for mutables as an optimization (e.g., list1 += list2 automatically calls list1.extend(list2), instead of the slower concatenation operation implied by +). Classes can overload in-place assignments with method names that begin with an i (e.g., __iadd__ for +=, __add__ for +). The format X //= Y (floor division) is new as of version 2.2.

Table 13. Augmented assignment statements

```
X += Y   X &= Y    X -= Y    X |= Y
X *= Y   X ^= Y    X /= Y    X >>= Y
X %= Y   X <<= Y   X **= Y   X //= Y
```

Normal and extended sequence assignment

In Python 2.X and 3.0, any sequence (or other iterable) of values may be assigned to any sequence of names, as long as the lengths are the same. This basic sequence assignment form works in most assignment contexts:

```
>>> a, b, c, d = [1, 2, 3, 4]
>>> a, d
(1, 4)

>>> for (a, b, c) in [[1, 2, 3], [4, 5, 6]]:
...     print(a, b, c)
...
1 2 3
4 5 6
```

In Python 3.0, sequence assignment is extended to allow collection of arbitrarily many items, by prefixing one variable in the assignment target with a star; when used, sequence lengths need not match:

```
>>> a, *b = [1, 2, 3, 4]
>>> a, b
(1, [2, 3, 4])

>>> a, *b, c = [1, 2, 3, 4]
>>> a, b, c
(1, [2, 3], 4)

>>> *a, b = [1, 2, 3, 4]
>>> a, b
([1, 2, 3], 4)

>>> for (a, *b) in [[1, 2, 3], [4, 5, 6]]: print(a, b)
...
1 [2, 3]
4 [5, 6]
```

The Expression Statement

```
expression
function([value, name=value, *name, **name...])
object.method([value, name=value, *name, **name...])
```

Any expression can appear on a line by itself as a statement (but statements cannot appear as expressions). Expressions are commonly used for calling functions and methods, and for interactive-mode printing. Expression statements are also the most common coding for `yield` expressions and Python 3.0 `print()` built-in function calls (though they are documented as specific statements in this book).

Call syntax

In function and method calls, actual arguments are separated by commas and are normally matched to arguments in function `def` headers by position. Calls can optionally list specific argument names in functions to receive passed values by using the `name=value` keyword argument syntax. Keyword arguments match by name instead of position.

Arbitrary arguments call syntax

Special syntax can be used in function and method call argument lists to unpack arbitrarily many arguments. If *pargs* and *kargs* are a sequence (or other iterable) and a dictionary, respectively:

```
f(*pargs, **kargs)
```

This format calls function `f` with positional arguments from iterable *pargs*, and keyword arguments from dictionary *kargs*. For instance:

```
>>> def f(a, b, c, d): print(a, b, c, d)
...
>>> f(*[1, 2], **dict(c=3, d=4))
1 2 3 4
```

This syntax is intended to be symmetric with function header arbitrary-argument syntax such as `def f(*pargs, **kargs)`. It is also flexible, since it can be easily combined with other positional and keyword arguments (e.g., `g(1, 2, foo=3, bar=4, *args, **kw)`).

In Python 2.X, the `apply()` built-in function achieves a similar effect but is removed as of Python 3.0:

```
apply(f, pargs, kargs)
```

See also "The def Statement" on page 64 for more call syntax details.

The print Statement

Printing takes the form of a built-in function call in Python 3.0, which is commonly coded as an expression statement (on a line by itself). Its call signature is as follows:

```
print([value [, value]*]
    [, sep=string] [, end=string] [, file=file])
```

Each `value` denotes an object to be printed. This call is configured by its three keyword-only arguments:

- `sep` is a string to place between values (defaults to a space: `' '`).
- `end` is a string to place at the end of the text printed (defaults to a newline: `'\n'`).
- `file` is the file-like object to which text is written (defaults to standard output: `sys.stdout`).

Pass empty or custom strings to suppress space separators and line feeds, and pass a file or file-like object to redirect output in your script:

```
>>> print(2 ** 32, 'spam')
4294967296 spam

>>> print(2 ** 32, 'spam', sep='')
4294967296spam

>>> print(2 ** 32, 'spam', end=' '); print(1, 2, 3)
4294967296 spam 1 2 3

>>> print(2 ** 32, 'spam', sep='', file=open('out', 'w'))
```

```
>>> open('out').read()
'4294967296spam\n'
```

Because by default **print** simply calls the **write** method of the object currently referenced by **sys.stdout**, the following is equivalent to **print(X)**:

```
import sys
sys.stdout.write(str(X) + '\n')
```

To redirect **print** text to files or class objects, either pass any object with a **write** method to the **file** keyword argument as shown earlier, or reassign **sys.stdout** to any such object:

```
sys.stdout = open('log', 'a')   # any object with a write()
print('Warning-bad spam!')      # goes to object's write()
```

Because **sys.stdout** can be reassigned, the **file** keyword argument is not strictly needed; however, it can often avoid both explicit **write** method calls, and saving and restoring the original **sys.stdout** value around a redirected **print** when the original stream is still required. See also "Built-in Functions" on page 102.

Python 2.X print statements

In Python 2.X, printing is a specific statement instead of a built-in function, of the following form:

```
print [value [, value]* [,]]
print >> file [, value [, value]* [,]]
```

The Python 2.X **print** statement displays the printable representation of values on the **stdout** stream (the current setting of **sys.stdout**) and adds spaces between values. The trailing comma suppresses the linefeed that is normally added at the end of a list, and is equivalent to using **end=' '** in Python 3.0:

```
>>> print 2 ** 32, 'spam'
4294967296 spam

>>> print 2 ** 32, 'spam',; print 1, 2, 3
4294967296 spam 1 2 3
```

The Python 2.X print statement can also name an open output file-like object to be the target of the printed text, instead of sys.stdout:

```
fileobj = open('log', 'a')
print >> fileobj, "Warning-bad spam!"
```

If the file object is None, sys.stdout is used. This Python 2.X >> syntax is equivalent to the file=F keyword argument in Python 3.0. There is no equivalent to sep=S in Python 2's statement.

To use the Python 3.0 printing function in Python 2.X, run the following:

```
from __future__ import print_function
```

The if Statement

```
if test:
    suite
[elif test:
    suite]*
[else:
    suite]
```

The if statement selects from among one or more actions (statement blocks), and it runs the suite associated with the first if or elif test that is true, or the else suite if all are false.

The while Statement

```
while test:
    suite
[else:
    suite]
```

The while loop is a general loop that keeps running the first suite while the test at the top is true. It runs the else suite if the loop exits without hitting a break statement.

The for Statement

```
for target in iterable:
    suite
[else:
    suite]
```

The for loop is a sequence (or other iterable) iteration that assigns items in *iterable* to *target* and runs the first suite for each. The for statement runs the else suite if the loop exits without hitting a break statement. *target* can be anything that can appear on the left side of an = assignment statement (e.g., for (x, y) in tuplelist:).

Since Python 2.2, this works by first trying to obtain an *iterator* object I with iter(*iterable*) and then calling that object's I.__next__() method repeatedly until StopIteration is raised (I.__next__() is named I.next() in Python 2); see "The yield Statement" on page 68 for more on iteration. In earlier versions, or if no iterator object can be obtained (e.g., no __iter__ method is defined), this works instead by repeatedly indexing *iterable* at successively higher offsets until an IndexError is raised.

The pass Statement

```
pass
```

This is a do-nothing placeholder statement, and is used when syntactically necessary. In Python 3.X only, ellipses (...) can achieve similar effects.

The break Statement

```
break
```

This immediately exits the closest enclosing while or for loop statement, skipping its associated else (if any).

The continue Statement

```
continue
```

This immediately goes to the top of the closest enclosing **while** or **for** loop statement; it resumes in the loop header line.

The del Statement

```
del name
del name[i]
del name[i:j:k]
del name.attribute
```

The **del** statement deletes names, items, slices, and attributes, as well as removes bindings. In the last three forms, *name* can actually be any expression (with parentheses if required for priority). For instance: **del a.b()[1].c.d**.

The def Statement

```
[decoration]
def name([arg,... arg=value,... *arg, **arg]):
    suite
```

The **def** statement makes new functions. It creates a function object and assigns it to variable *name*. Each call to a function object generates a new, local scope, where assigned names are local to the function call by default (unless declared global). See also the section "Namespace and Scope Rules" on page 82. Arguments are passed by assignment; in a **def** header, they can be defined by any of the four formats in Table 14.

The argument forms in Table 14 can also be used in a function call, where they are interpreted as shown in Table 15 (see "The Expression Statement" on page 59 for more on function call syntax).

Table 14. Argument formats in definitions

Argument format	Interpretation
arg	Matched by name or position
arg=value	Default value if arg is not passed
*arg	Collects extra positional args as a new tuple
**arg	Collects extra keyword args passed as a new dictionary
*name, arg[=value]	Python 3.0 keyword-only arguments after *
*, arg[=value]	Same as prior line

Table 15. Argument formats in calls

Argument format	Interpretation
arg	Positional argument
arg=value	Keyword (match by name) argument
*arg	Sequence (or other iterable) of positional arguments
**arg	Dictionary of keyword arguments

Python 3.0 keyword-only arguments

Python 3.0 generalizes function definition to allow keyword-only arguments, which must be passed by keyword, and are required if not coded with defaults. Keyword-only arguments are coded after the *, which may appear without a name if there are keyword-only arguments but not arbitrary positionals:

```
>>> def f(a, *b, c): print(a, b, c)   # c required keyword
...
>>> f(1, 2, c=3)
1 (2,) 3

>>> def f(a, *, c=None): print(a, c) # c optional keyword
...
>>> f(1)
1 None
>>> f(1, c='spam')
1 spam
```

Python 3.0 function annotations

Python 3.0 also generalizes function definition to allow arguments and return values to be annotated with object values for use in extensions. Annotations are coded as :value after the argument name and before a default, and ->value after the argument list. They are collected into an __annotations__ attribute, but are not otherwise treated as special by Python itself:

```
>>> def f(a:99, b:'spam'=None) -> float:
...     print(a, b)
...
>>> f(88)
88 None
>>> f.__annotations__
{'a': 99, 'b': 'spam', 'return': <class 'float'>}
```

lambda expressions

Functions can also be created with the lambda expression form which creates a new function object and returns it to be called later, instead of assigning it to a name:

```
lambda arg, arg,...: expression
```

In lambda, *arg* is as in def, *expression* is the implied return value of later calls. Because lambda is an expression, not a statement, it can be used in places that a def cannot (e.g., within a dictionary literal expression, or an argument list of a function call). Because lambda computes a single expression instead of running statements, it is not intended for complex functions.

Defaults and attributes

Mutable default argument values are evaluated once at def statement time, not on each call, and so can retain state between calls. However, some consider this behavior to be a caveat, and classes and enclosing scope references are often better state-retention tools; use None defaults for mutable and explicit tests to avoid changes as shown in the following's comments:

```
>>> def grow(a, b=[]):      # ..., b=None)
...     b.append(a)         # if b == None: b = []
...     print(b)
```

```
   ...
>>> grow(1); grow(2)
[1]
[1, 2]
```

Both Python 2.X and 3.0 also support attachment of arbitrary attributes to functions, as another form of state retention (though attributes support only per-function-object state, which is only per-call if each call generates a new function):

```
>>> grow.food = 'spam'
>>> grow.food
'spam'
```

Function and method decorators

As of Python 2.4, function definitions can be preceded by a declaration syntax that describes the function that follows. Known as *decorators* and coded with an @ character, these declarations provide explicit syntax for functional techniques. The function decorator syntax:

```
@decorator
def F():
    ...
```

is equivalent to this manual name rebinding:

```
def F():
    ...
F = decorator(F)
```

The effect is to rebind the function name to the result of passing the function through the decorator callable. Function decorators may be used to manage functions, or later calls made to them (by using proxy objects). Decorators may be applied to any function definition, including methods inside a class:

```
class C:
    @decorator
    def M():             # same as M = decorator(M)
        ...
```

More generally, the following nested decoration:

```
@A
@B
```

```
@C
def f(): ...
```

is equivalent to the following nondecorator code:

```
def f(): ...
f = A(B(C(f)))
```

Decorators may also take argument lists:

```
@spam(1,2,3)
def f(): ...
```

In this case `spam` must be a function returning a function (known as a *factory function*); its result is used as the actual decorator. Decorators must appear on the line before a function definition, and cannot be on the same line (e.g., `@A def f(): ...` is illegal).

Because they accept and return callables, some built-in functions, including `property()`, `staticmethod()`, and `classmethod()`, may be used as function decorators (see "Built-in Functions" on page 102). Decorator syntax is also supported for classes in Python 2.6 and 3.0 and later; see "The class Statement" on page 73.

The return Statement

```
return [expression]
```

The `return` statement exits the enclosing function and returns an *expression* value as the result of the call to the function. The *expression* defaults to `None` if it's omitted. Hint: return a tuple for multiple-value function results.

The yield Statement

```
yield expression
```

The `yield` expression, commonly coded as an expression statement (on a line by itself), suspends function state and returns an *expression*. On the next iteration, the function's prior state is restored, and control resumes immediately after the `yield`

---

statement. Use a `return` statement with no value to end the iteration, or simply fall off the end of the function:

```
def generateSquares(N):
    for i in range(N):
        yield i ** 2

>>> G = generateSquares(5)
>>> list(G)                      # force results generation
[0, 1, 4, 9, 16]
```

When used as an expression, `yield` returns the object passed to the generator's `send()` method at the caller (e.g., `A = yield X`), and must be enclosed in parenthesis unless it is the only item on the right of `=` (e.g., `A = (yield X) + 42`). In this mode, values are sent to a generator by calling `send(value)`; the generator is resumed, and the `yield` expression returns `value`. If the regular `__next__()` method or `next()` built-in function is called to advance, `yield` returns `None`.

Generators also have a `throw(type)` method to raise an exception inside the generator at the latest `yield`, and a `close()` method that raises a new `GeneratorExit` exception inside the generator to terminate the iteration. `yield` is standard as of version 2.3 and later; generator `send()`, `throw()`, and `close()` methods are available as of Python 2.5.

Generators and iterators

Functions containing a `yield` statement are compiled as *generators*; when called, they return a generator object that supports the iterator protocol to produce results on demand. *Iterators* are objects returned by the `iter(X)` built-in function; they define a `__next__()` method, which returns the next item in the iteration or raises a `StopIteration` exception to end the iteration.

All iteration contexts including `for` loops and comprehensions automatically use the iteration protocol to step through collections. In addition, the `next(I)` built-in function automatically calls `I.__next__()` to simplify manual iteration loops.

Classes can provide an __iter__() method to intercept the iter(X) built-in function call; if defined, its result has a __next__() method used to step through results in iteration contexts. If no __iter__() is defined, the __getitem__() indexing method is used as a fallback to iterate until IndexError.

In Python 2.X, the I.__next__() method is named I.next(), but iteration works the same otherwise. The next() function calls the I.next() method in 2.6. See also "Generator expressions" on page 39 for related tools.

The global Statement

```
global name [, name]*
```

The global statement is a namespace declaration: when used inside a class or function definition statement, it causes all appearances of *name* in that context to be treated as references to a global (module-level) variable of that name—whether name is assigned or not, and whether name already exists or not.

This statement allows globals to be created or changed within a function or class. Because of Python's scope rules, you need to declare only global names that are assigned; undeclared names are made local if assigned, but global references are automatically located in the enclosing module. See also "Namespace and Scope Rules" on page 82.

The nonlocal Statement

```
nonlocal name [, name]*
```

Available in Python 3.0 only.

The nonlocal statement is a namespace declaration: when used inside a nested function, it causes all appearances of *name* in that context to be treated as references to a local variable of that name in an enclosing function's scope—whether name is assigned or not.

name must exist in an enclosing function; this statement allows it to be changed by a nested function. Because of Python's scope rules, you need to declare only nonlocal names that are assigned; undeclared names are made local if assigned, but nonlocal references are automatically located in enclosing functions. See also "Namespace and Scope Rules" on page 82.

The import Statement

```
import module [, module]*
import [package.]* module [, [package.]* module]*
import [package.]* module as name
              [, [package.]*module as name]*
```

The **import** statement provides module access: it imports a module as a whole. Modules in turn contain names fetched by qualification (e.g., *module.attribute*). Assignments at the top level of a Python file create module object attributes. The **as** clause assigns a variable *name* to the imported module object; it is useful to provide shorter synonyms for long module names.

module names the target module—usually a Python source file or compiled module—which must be located in a directory in **sys.path**. The **module** is given without its filename suffix (.*py* and other extensions are omitted). The **sys.path** module import search path is a directory list initialized from the program's top-level directory, **PYTHONPATH** settings, **.pth** path file contents, and Python defaults.

Import operations compile a file's source to byte-code if needed (and save it in a .*pyc* file if possible), then execute the compiled code from top to bottom to generate module object attributes by assignment. Use the **imp.reload()** built-in function to force recompilation and execution of already-loaded modules; see also **__import__** used by **import** in the section "Built-in Functions" on page 102.

In the Jython implementation, imports can also name Java class libraries; Jython generates a Python module wrapper that interfaces with the Java library. In standard CPython, imports can also load compiled C and C++ extensions.

Package imports

If used, the *package* prefix names give enclosing directory names, and module dotted paths reflect directory hierarchies. An import of the form `import dir1.dir2.mod` generally loads the module file at directory path *dir1/dir2/mod.py*, where *dir1* must be contained by a directory listed on the module search path `sys.path`.

Each directory listed in an import statement must have a (possibly empty) `__init__.py` file that serves as the directory level's module namespace. This file is run on the first import through the directory, and all names assigned in `__init__.py` files become attributes of the directory's module object. Directory packages can resolve conflicts caused by the linear nature of `PYTHONPATH`.

See also "Package relative import syntax" on page 73.

The from Statement

```
from [package.]* module import name [, name]*
from [package.]* module import *
from [package.]* module import name as othername
from [package.]* module import (name1, name2, ...)
```

The `from` statement imports variable names from a module so that you can use those names later without the need to qualify them with their module name. The `from mod import *` format copies *all* names assigned at the top level of the module, except names with a single leading underscore or names not listed in the module's `__all__` list-of-strings attribute (if defined).

If used, the `as` clause creates a name synonym. If used, *package* import paths work the same as in `import` statements (e.g., `from dir1.dir2.mod import X`), but the package path needs to be listed only in the `from` itself. Due to new scoping rules, the `*` format generates warnings in version 2.2 if it appears nested in a function or class (this generates errors in Python 3.0).

As of Python 2.4, the names being imported from a module can be enclosed in parentheses to span multiple lines without backslashes. As of Python 3.0, `from module import *` form is invalid within a function, because it makes it impossible to classify name scopes at definition time.

The `from` statement is also used to enable future (but still experimental) language additions, with `from __future__ import` *featurename*. This format must appear only at the top of a module file (preceded only by an optional doc string).

Package relative import syntax

In Python 3.0, the `from` statement (but not `import`) may use leading dots in module names to specify that imports be relative to the package directory in which the importing module resides:

```
from module import name [, name]*      # sys.path: abs
from . import module [, module]*       # pkg dir only: rel
from .module import name [, name]*     # pkg dir only: rel
from .. import module [, module]*      # parent dir in pkg
from ..module import name [, name]*    # parent dir in pkg
```

The leading-dots syntax works to make imports explicitly package-relative in both Python 3.0 and 2.6. For imports without the dots syntax, the package's own directory is searched first in Python 2.6, but not in Python 3.0. To enable Python 3.0 package import semantics in Python 2.6, use:

```
from __future__ import absolute_import
```

Absolute package imports, relative to a directory on `sys.path`, are generally preferred over both implicit package-relative imports in Python 2.X, and explicit package-relative import syntax in both Python 2.X and 3.0.

The class Statement

```
[decoration]
class name [ ( super [, super]* [, metaclass=M] ) ]:
    suite
```

The `class` statement makes new class objects, which are factories for instance objects. The new class object inherits from each listed **super** class in the order given, and is assigned to variable *name*. The `class` statement introduces a new local name scope, and all names assigned in the `class` statement generate class object attributes shared by all instances of the class.

Important class features include the following (see also the sections "Object-Oriented Programming" on page 85 and "Operator Overloading Methods" on page 88):

- Superclasses (also known as base classes) from which a new class inherits attributes are listed in parentheses in the header (e.g., class Sub(Super1, Super2):).

- Assignments in the suite generate class attributes inherited by instances: nested `def` statements make methods, while assignment statements make simple class members, etc.

- Calling the class generates instance objects. Each instance object may have its own attributes, and inherits the attributes of the class and all of its superclasses.

- Method functions receive a special first argument, usually called **self**, which is the instance object that is the implied subject of the method call, and gives access to instance state information attributes.

- Specially named __X__ method definitions intercept built-in operations.

Class decorators in Python 2.6 and 3.0

In Python 2.6, 3.0, and later, decorator syntax can be applied to class statements, in addition to function definitions. The class decorator syntax:

```
@decorator
class C:
    def meth():
        ...
```

is equivalent to this manual name rebinding:

```
class C:
    def meth():
        ...
C = decorator(C)
```

The effect is to rebind the class name to the result of passing the class through the decorator callable. Like function decorators, class decorators may be nested and support decorator arguments. Class decorators may be used to manage classes, or later instance-creation calls made to them (by using proxy objects).

Metaclasses

Metaclasses are classes that generally subclass from the type class, in order to customize creation of class objects themselves:

```
class Meta(type):
    def __new__(meta, cname, supers, cdict):
        # run by inherited type.__call__
        return type.__new__(meta, cname, supers, cdict)
```

In Python 3.0, classes define their metaclasses using keyword arguments in **class** headers:

```
class C(metaclass=Meta): ...
```

In Python 2.X, use class attributes instead:

```
class C:
    __metaclass__ = Meta
    ...
```

See also **type()** in "Built-in Functions" on page 102 for the mapping from class statements.

The try Statement

```
try:
    suite
except [type [as value]]:        # [, value] in Python 2
    suite
[except [type [as value]]:
```

```
    suite]*
[else:
    suite]
[finally:
    suite]

try:
    suite
finally:
    suite
```

The **try** statement catches exceptions. **try** statements can specify **except** clauses with suites that serve as handlers for exceptions raised during the **try** suite, **else** clauses that run if no exception occurs during the **try** suite, and **finally** clauses that run whether an exception happens or not. **except** clauses catch and recover from exceptions, and **finally** clauses define termination actions.

Exceptions can be raised by Python, or explicitly (see also the **raise** statement discussed in the next section, "The raise Statement" on page 78). In **except** clauses, *type* is an expression giving the exception class to be caught, and an extra variable name *value* can be used to intercept the instance of the exception class that was raised. Table 16 lists all the clauses that can appear in a **try** statement.

The **try** must have either an **except** or a **finally**, or both. The order of its parts must be: try→except→else→finally, where the **else** and **finally** are optional, and there may be zero or more **except**, but there must be at least one **except** if an **else** appears. **finally** interacts correctly with **return**, **break**, and **continue** (if any of these pass control out of the **try** block, the **finally** clause is executed on the way out).

Table 16. try statement clause formats

Clause format	Interpretation
except:	Catch all (or all other) exceptions
except *type*:	Catch a specific exception only

Clause format	Interpretation
except *type* as *value*:	Catch exception and its instance
except (*type1*, *type2*):	Catch any of the exceptions
except (*type1*, *type2*) as *value*:	Catch any of the exceptions and its instance
else:	Run if no exceptions are raised
finally:	Always run this block on the way out

Common variations include the following:

except *classname* as X:

> Catch a class exception, and assign X to the raised instance. X gives access to any attached state information attributes, print strings, or callable methods on the instance raised. For older string exceptions, X is assigned to the extra data passed along with the string (string exceptions are removed in Python 3.0 and 2.6).

except (*type1*, *type2*, *type3*) as X:

> Catch any of the exceptions named in a tuple, and assign X to the extra data.

See also the sys.exc_info() call in "The sys Module" on page 133 for generic access to the exception class and instance (a.k.a., type and value) after an exception is raised.

Python 2.X try statement forms

In Python 2.X, try statements work as described, but the as clause used in except handlers to access the raised instance is coded with a comma instead:

except *classname*, X:

> Catch a class exception, and assign X to the raised instance.

except (*name1*, *name2*, *name2*), X:

> Catch any of the exceptions, and assign X to the extra data.

The raise Statement

In Python 3.0, the `raise` statement takes the following forms:

`raise instance [from otherexc]`
> Raise a manually created instance of a class (e.g., `raise Error(args)`).

`raise class [from otherexc]`
> Make and raise a new instance of `class` (equivalent to `raise class()`).

`raise`
> Re-raise the most recent exception.

The `raise` statement triggers exceptions. You can use it to explicitly raise either built-in exceptions, or user-defined exceptions. Without arguments, `raise` re-raises the most recent exception. See also "Built-in Exceptions" on page 124 for exceptions raised by Python.

On a `raise`, control jumps to the matching `except` clause of the most recently entered matching `try` statement, or to the top level of the process (where it ends the program and prints a standard error message). The instance object raised is assigned to the `as` variable in the matching `except` clause (if given).

The optional `from` clause allows exception chaining in Python 3.0 (only): *otherexc* is another exception class or instance, and is attached to the raised exception's `__cause__` attribute. If the raised exception is not caught, Python prints both exceptions as part of the standard error message.

Class exceptions

In Python 3.0 and 2.6 all exceptions are identified by classes, which must be derived from the built-in `Exception` class (in 2.6 this derivation is required of new-style classes only). The `Exception` superclass provides default display strings and constructor argument retention in tuple attribute `args`.

Class exceptions support exception *categories*, which can be easily extended. Because **try** statements catch all subclasses when they name a superclass, exception categories can be modified by altering the set of subclasses without breaking existing **try** statements. The raised instance object also provides storage for extra information about the exception:

```
class General(Exception):
    def __init__(self, x):
        self.data = x

class Specific1(General): pass
class Specific2(General): pass

try:
    raise Specific1('spam')
except General as X:
    print(X.data)                # prints 'spam'
```

Python 2.X raise statement forms

Prior to Python 2.6, Python 2.X allows exceptions to be identified with both strings and classes. Because of this, its raise statements may take the following forms, many of which exist for backward compatibility:

raise *string*

> Matches an **except** handler clause that names the raised string object.

raise *string, data*

> Passes an extra *data* object with an exception (the default is **None**); it is assigned to variable X in an **except string, X: try** statement clause.

raise *instance*

> This is the same as **raise instance.__class__, instance**.

raise *class, instance*

> Matches an **except** that names this *class*, or any of its superclasses. Passes the class *instance* object as extra exception data, to be assigned to X in an **except** *class, X:*.

```
raise class
```
Same as `raise class()` (makes an instance of class).

```
raise class, arg
```
Same as `raise class(arg)` (makes an instance of class from non-instance arg).

```
raise class, (arg [, arg]*)
```
Same as `raise class(arg, arg, ...)` (makes an instance of class).

```
raise
```
Re-raises the current exception.

String exceptions were deprecated as of (and issues warnings in) Python 2.5. Python 2.X also allows a third item in `raise` statements, which must be a traceback object used instead of the current location as the place where the exception occurred.

The assert Statement

```
assert expression [, message]
```

The **assert** statement performs debugging checks. If *expression* is false, it raises **AssertionError**, passing *message* as an extra data item if specified. The -0 command-line flag removes assertions (their tests are not run).

The with Statement

```
with expression [as variable]:        # Python 2.6 and 3.0
    suite

with expression [as variable]
        [, expression [as variable]]*:  # 3.1
    suite
```

The **with** statement wraps a nested block of code in a context manager, which ensures that block entry and/or exit actions are run. This is an alternative to **try**/**finally** for objects having context managers that perform termination actions whether exceptions are raised or not.

expression is assumed to return an object that supports the context management protocol. This object may also return a value that will be assigned to the name *variable* if the optional **as** clause is present. Classes may define custom context managers, and some built-in types such as files and threads provide context managers with exit actions that close files, release thread locks, etc.:

```
with open(r'C:\misc\script', 'w') as myfile:
    ...process myfile, auto-closed on statement exit...
```

See "Files" on page 45 for more details on file context manager usage, and Python manuals for other built-in types that support this protocol and statement, as well as details on the protocol itself.

This statement is supported as of Python 2.6 and 3.0, and may be enabled in 2.5 with the following:

```
from __future__ import with_statement
```

Multiple context managers in Python 3.1

In Python 3.1, this statement may also specify multiple (a.k.a. nested) context managers. Any number of context manager items may be separated by commas, and multiple items work the same as nested **with** statements. In general, the 3.1 and later code:

```
with A() as a, B() as b:
    ...statements...
```

is equivalent to the following, which works in 3.1, 3.0, and 2.6:

```
with A() as a:
    with B() as b:
        ...statements...
```

For example, in the following code both files' exit actions are automatically run when the statement block exits, regardless of exception outcomes:

```
with open('data') as fin, open('results', 'w') as fout:
    for line in fin:
        fout.write(transform(line))
```

Python 2.X Statements

Python 2.X supports the **print** statement described above, does not support **nonlocal**, and does not support **with** until 2.6. In addition, **raise**, **try**, and **def** have the slightly different syntaxes in Python 2.X as noted above.

The following additional statement is available in Python 2.X only:

```
exec codestring [in globaldict [, localdict]]
```

The **exec** statement compiles and runs code strings. *codestring* is any Python statement (or multiple statements separated by newlines) as a string; it is run in a namespace containing the **exec**, or the global/local namespace dictionaries if specified (*localdict* defaults to *globaldict*). *codestring* can also be a compiled code object. Also see **compile()**, **eval()**, and the Python 2.X **execfile()** in "Built-in Functions" on page 102.

In Python 3.0, this statement becomes the **exec()** function (see "Built-in Functions" on page 102). The backward- and forward-compatible syntax **exec(a, b, c)** is also accepted in Python 2.

Namespace and Scope Rules

This section discusses rules for name binding and lookup (see also the sections "Name format" on page 54 and "Name conventions" on page 55). In all cases, names are created when first assigned but must already exist when referenced. Qualified and unqualified names are resolved differently.

Qualified Names: Object Namespaces

Qualified names (X, in **object.X**) are known as *attributes* and live in object namespaces. Assignments in some lexical scopes[§] initialize object namespaces (modules, classes).

`Assignment: object.X = value`
> Creates or alters the attribute name X in the namespace of the **object** being qualified.

`Reference: object.X`
> Searches for the attribute name X in the **object**, then all accessible classes above it (for instances and classes). This is the definition of *inheritance*.

Unqualified Names: Lexical Scopes

Unqualified names (X) involve lexical scope rules. Assignments bind such names to the local scope unless they are declared global.

`Assignment: X = value`
> Makes name X local by default: creates or changes name X in the current local scope. If X is declared **global**, this creates or changes name X in the enclosing module's scope. If X is declared **nonlocal** in Python 3.0, this changes name X in an enclosing function's scope. Local variables are stored in the call stack at runtime for quick access.

`Reference: X`
> Looks for name X in at most four scope categories: in the current *local* scope (function); then in the local scopes of all lexically *enclosing functions* (if any, from inner to outer); then in the current *global* scope (module); then in the *built-in* scope (which corresponds to module **builtins** in Python 3.0, and module **__builtin__** in Python 2.X). Local and global scope contexts are defined in Table 17. **global** declarations make the search begin in the

[§] Lexical scopes refer to physically (syntactically) nested code structures in a program's source code.

global scope instead, and `nonlocal` declarations restrict the search to enclosing functions.

Table 17. Unqualified name scopes

Code context	Global scope	Local scope
Module	Same as local	The module itself
Function, method	Enclosing module	Function call
Class	Enclosing module	`class` statement
Script, interactive mode	Same as local	module `__main__`
`exec()`, `eval()`	Caller's global (or passed in)	Caller's local (or passed in)

Statically Nested Scopes

The *enclosing functions* search of the last rule in the previous section (`Reference: X`) is called a *statically nested scope*, and was made standard in version 2.2. For example, the following function now works because the reference to x within f2 has access to the scope of f1:

```
def f1():
    x = 42
    def f2():
        print(x)
    f2()
```

In Python versions prior to 2.2, this function fails because name x is not local (in f2's scope), global (in the module enclosing f1), or built-in. To make such cases work prior to version 2.2, default arguments retain values from the immediately enclosing scope (defaults are evaluated before entering a `def`):

```
def f1():
    x = 42
    def f2(x=x):
        print(x)
    f2()
```

This rule also applies to `lambda` expressions, which imply a nested scope just like `def` and are more commonly nested in practice:

```
def func(x):
    action = (lambda n: x ** n)         # works as of 2.2
    return action

def func(x):
    action = (lambda n, x=x: x ** n)    # use before 2.2
    return action
```

Defaults are still sometimes needed to reference loop variables when creating functions inside loops (they reflect their final loop value). Scopes nest arbitrarily, but only enclosing functions (not classes) are searched:

```
def f1():
    x = 42
    def f2():
        def f3():
            print(x)    # found in f1's scope
        f3()
    f2()
```

Object-Oriented Programming

Classes are Python's main object-oriented programming (OOP) tool. They support multiple instances, attribute inheritance, and operator overloading.

Classes and Instances

Class objects provide default behavior

- The `class` statement creates a *class* object and assigns it to a name.
- Assignments inside `class` statements create class *attributes*, which are inherited object state and behavior.
- Class *methods* are nested `def`s, with special first arguments to receive the implied subject instance.

Instance objects are generated from classes

- Calling a class object like a function makes a new *instance* object.
- Each instance object inherits class attributes and gets its own attribute *namespace*.
- Assignments to attributes of the first argument (e.g., `self.X = V`) in methods create per-instance *attributes*.

Inheritance rules

- Inheritance happens at attribute qualification time: on `object.attribute`, if `object` is a class or instance.
- Classes inherit attributes from all classes listed in their class statement header line (superclasses). Listing more than one means *multiple inheritance*.
- Instances inherit attributes from the class from which they are generated, plus all that class's superclasses.
- Inheritance searches the instance, then its class, then all accessible superclasses, and uses the first version of an attribute name found. Superclasses are searched depth-first and then left-to-right (but new-style classes search across before proceeding up in diamond pattern trees).

Pseudoprivate Attributes

By default, all attribute names in modules and classes are visible everywhere. Special conventions allow some limited data-hiding but are mostly designed to prevent name collisions (see also the section "Name conventions" on page 55).

Module privates

Names in modules with a single underscore (e.g., `_X`), and those not listed on the module's `__all__` list, are not copied over when a client uses `from module import *`. This is not strict privacy, though, as such names can still be accessed with other import statement forms.

Class privates

Names anywhere within `class` statements with two leading underscores only (e.g., `__X`) are mangled at compile time to include the enclosing class name as a prefix (e.g., `_Class__X`). The added class-name prefix localizes such names to the enclosing class and thus makes them distinct in both the `self` instance object and the class hierarchy.

This helps to avoid clashes that may arise for same-named methods, and for attributes in the single instance object at the bottom of the inheritance chain (all assignments to `self.attr` anywhere in a framework change the single instance namespace). This is not strict privacy, though, as such attributes can still be accessed via the mangled name.

New Style Classes

In Python 3.0, there is a single class model: all classes are considered new-style whether they derive from `object` or not. In Python 2.X, there are two class models: *classic* (the default), and *new-style* in version 2.2 and later (coded by deriving from a built-in type or `object`—`class A(object)`).

New-style classes (and all classes in Python 3.0) differ from classic classes in the following ways:

- Diamond patterns of multiple inheritances have a slightly different search order—roughly, they are searched across before up, and more breadth-first than depth-first.

- Classes are now types, and types are now classes. The `type(I)` built-in returns the class an instance is made from, instead of a generic instance type, and is normally the same as `I.__class__`. The `type` class may be subclassed to customize class creation, and all classes inherit from `object`.

- The `__getattr__` and `__getattribute__` methods are no longer run for attributes implicitly fetched by built-in operations. They are not called for `__X__` operator -overloading method names; the search for such names begins at classes, not instances. To intercept and delegate access to such method names, they generally must be redefined in wrapper/proxy classes.

- New-style classes have a set of new class tools, including slots, properties, descriptors, and the `__getattribute__` method. Most of these have tool-building purposes. See the next section "Operator Overloading Methods" for `__slots__`, `__getattribute__`, and descriptor `__get__`, `__set__`, and `__delete__` methods; see "Built-in Functions" on page 102 for `property()`.

Operator Overloading Methods

Classes intercept and implement built-in operations by providing specially named method functions, all of which start and end with two underscores. These names are not reserved and can be inherited from superclasses as usual. Python locates and calls at most one per operation.

Python automatically calls a class's overloading methods when instances appear in expressions and other contexts. For example, if a class defines a method named `__getitem__`, and X is an instance of this class, the expression X[i] is equivalent to the method call X.`__getitem__`(i).

Overloading method names are sometimes arbitrary: a class's `__add__` method need not perform an addition (or concatenation). Moreover, classes generally can mix numeric and collection methods and mutable and immutable operations. Most operator overloading names have no defaults, and the corresponding operation raises an exception if its method is not defined.

For All Types

`__new__`(cls [, args...])
    Called to create and return a new instance of class `cls`. Receives constructor arguments passed to the class. If this

returns an instance of the class, the instance's `__init__` method is invoked with the same constructor arguments. Not used in normal classes; intended to allow subclasses of immutable types to customize instance creation, and to allow custom metaclasses to customize class creation.

`__init__(self [, arg]*)`

Invoked on `class(args...)`. This is the constructor that initializes the new instance, `self`. When run for calls to a class name, `self` is provided automatically; `arg` is the arguments passed to the class name, and may be any function-definition argument form (see "The Expression Statement" on page 59 and "The def Statement" on page 64). Must return no value, and call superclass `__init__` manually if needed, passing the instance to `self`.

`__del__(self)`

Invoked on instance garbage collection. This destructor method cleans up when an instance is freed. Embedded objects are automatically freed when the parent is (unless referenced from elsewhere). Exceptions during this method's run are ignored, and simply print messages to `sys.stderr`. The `try`/`finally` statement allows more predictable termination actions for a code block.

`__repr__(self)`

Invoked on `repr(self)`, and interactive echoes, (and `` `self` `` in Python 2.X only). Also invoked on `str(self)` and `print(self)` if there is no `__str__`. This method returns a low-level "as code" string representation of `self`.

`__str__(self)`

Invoked on `str(self)` and `print(self)` (or uses `__repr__` as a backup if defined). This method returns a high-level "user friendly" string representation of `self`.

`__format__(self, formatspec)`

Called by the `format()` built-in function (and by extension, the `str.format()` method of `str` strings) to produce a "formatted" string representation of an object. See

"Strings" on page 19 and "Built-in Functions" on page 102. New in Python 2.6 and 3.0.

__hash__(self)

Invoked on dictionary[self] and hash(self), and other hashed collection operations, including those of the set object type. This method returns a unique and unchanging integer hash-key.

__bool__(self)

Called for truth value testing and the built-in bool() function; returns False or True. When __bool__() is not defined, __len__() is called if it is defined and designates a true value with a nonzero length. If neither __len__() nor __bool__() is defined, all its instances are considered true. New in Python 3.0; in Python 2.X, this method is named __nonzero__ instead of __bool__, but works the same way.

__call__(self [, arg]*)

Invoked on self(args...), when an instance is called like a function. arg may take any function-definition argument form (see "The Expression Statement" on page 59 and "The def Statement" on page 64). For example, __call__(self, a, b, c, d=5) and __call__(self, *pargs, **kargs) both match calls self(1, 2, 3, 4) and self(1, *(2,), c=3, **dict(d=4)).

__getattr__(self, name)

Invoked on self.name, when name is an undefined attribute access (this method is not called if name exists in or is inherited by self). name is a string. This method returns an object or raises AttributeError.

In Python 3.0, this is no longer run for __X__ attributes implicitly fetched by built-in operations; redefine such names in wrapper/proxy classes.

__setattr__(self, name, value)

Invoked on self.name=value (all attribute assignments). Hint—assign through __dict__ key to avoid recursive loops: self.attr=x statement within a __setattr__ calls __setattr__ again, but self.__dict__['attr']=x does not. Recursion may also be avoided by calling the super-class version explicitly: `object.__setattr__(self, name, value)`.

`__delattr__(self, name)`

Invoked on `del self.name` (all attribute deletions). Hint: must avoid recursive loops by routing attribute deletions through `__dict__` or a superclass, much like `__setattr__`.

`__getattribute__(self, name)`

Called unconditionally to implement attribute accesses for instances of the class. If the class also defines `__getattr__`, it will never be called (unless it is called explicitly). This method should return the (computed) attribute value or raise an `AttributeError` exception. To avoid infinite recursion in this method, its implementation should always call the superclass method with the same name to access any attributes it needs (e.g., `object.__getattribute__(self, name)`).

In Python 3.0, this is no longer run for `__X__` attributes implicitly fetched by built-in operations; redefine such names in wrapper/proxy classes.

`__lt__(self, other)`,
`__le__(self, other)`,
`__eq__(self, other)`,
`__ne__(self, other)`,
`__gt__(self, other)`,
`__ge__(self, other)`

Respectively, used on `self < other`, `self <= other`, `self == other`, `self != other`, and `self > other`, `self >= other`. Added in version 2.1, these are known as *rich comparison* methods and are called for all comparison expressions in Python 3.0. For example, `X < Y` calls `X.__lt__(Y)` if defined. In Python 2.X only, these methods are called in preference to `__cmp__`, and `__ne__` is also run for `self <> other`.

These methods can return any value, but if the comparison operator is used in a Boolean context, the return value is interpreted as a Boolean result for the operator. These methods can also return (not raise) the special object `NotImplemented` if not supported for the operands (which works as though the method were not defined at all, and which forces Python 2.X to revert to the general `__cmp__` method if defined).

There are no implied relationships among comparison operators. For example, `x==y` being true does not imply that `x!=y` is false: `__ne__` should be defined along with `__eq__` if the operators are expected to behave symmetrically. There are also no right-side (swapped-argument) versions of these methods to be used when the left argument does not support the operation but the right argument does. `__lt__` and `__gt__` are each other's reflection, `__le__` and `__ge__` are each other's reflection, and `__eq__` and `__ne__` are their own reflections. Use `__lt__` for sorting in Python 3.0.

`__slots__`

This class attribute can be assigned a string, iterable, or sequence of strings giving the names of attributes of instances of the class. If defined in a new-style class (including all classes in Python 3), `__slots__` reserves space for the declared attributes, and prevents the automatic creation of `__dict__` for each instance (unless string `'__dict__'` is included in `__slots__`, in which case instances also have a `__dict__` and attributes not named in `__slots__` may be added dynamically).

To support classes with `__slots__`, tools that generically list attribute or access then by string name must use storage-neutral tools such as the `getattr()`, `setattr()`, and `dir()`, which apply to both `__dict__` and `__slots__` attribute storage. Both attribute sources may need to be queried.

`__dir__(self)`

Called on `dir(self)`. Returns a list of attribute names. New in Python 3.0.

For Collections (Sequences, Mappings)

__len__(self)

> Invoked on len(self) and possibly for truth-value tests. This method returns a collection's size. For Boolean tests, Python looks for __bool__ first, then __len__, and then considers the object true (__bool__ is named __nonzero__ in Python 2). Zero length means false.

__contains__(self, item)

> Invoked on item in self for custom membership tests (otherwise, membership uses __iter__, if defined, or __getitem__). This method returns a true or false result.

__iter__(self)

> Invoked on iter(self). New in version 2.2, this method is part of the iteration protocol. It returns an object with a __next__() method (possibly self). The result object's __next__() method is then called repeatedly in all iteration contexts (e.g., for loops), and should return the next result or raise StopIteration to terminate the results progression. See also sections "The for Statement" on page 63 and "The yield Statement" on page 68. If no __iter__ is defined, iteration falls back on __getitem__. In Python 2.X, __next__() is named next().

__next__(self)

> Invoked by the next(self) built-in function, and by all iteration contexts to advance through results. See __iter__() for usage details. New in Python 3.0; in Python 2.X, this method is named next(), but works the same way.

__getitem__(self, key)

> Invoked on self[key], self[i:j:k], x in self, and for x in self (and all iteration contexts). This method implements all indexing-related operations. Iteration contexts (e.g., in and for) repeatedly index from 0 until IndexError, unless __iter__ is defined.

In Python 3.0, this and the following two methods are also called for slice operations, in which case `key` is a slice object. Slice objects may be propagated to another slice expression, and have attributes `start`, `stop`, and `step`, any of which can be `None`. See also `slice()` in "Built-in Functions" on page 102.

`__setitem__(self, key, value)`
> Invoked on `self[key]=value`, `self[i:j:k]=value`. This method is called for assignment to a collection key or index, or to a sequence's slice.

`__delitem__(self, key)`
> Invoked on `del self[key]`, `del self[i:j:k]`. This method called is for index/key and sequence slice deletion.

`__reversed__(self)`
> Called if defined by the `reversed()` built-in function to implement custom reverse iteration. Returns a new iterator object that iterates over all the objects in the container in reverse order. If no `__reversed__` is defined, `reversed()` expects and uses sequence protocol (methods `__len__()` and `__getitem__()`).

For Numbers (Binary Operators)

If one of those methods does not support the operation with the supplied arguments, it should return (not raise) the built-in `NotImplemented` object (which works as though the method were not defined at all).

Basic binary methods

`__add__(self, other)`
> Invoked on `self + other` for numeric addition or sequence concatenation.

__sub__(self, other)
> Invoked on self - other.

__mul__(self, other)
> Invoked on self * other for numeric multiplication or sequence repetition.

__truediv__(self, other)
> Invoked on self / other for all division (which retains remainders) in Python 3.0. In Python 2.X only, __div__ is called for classic division (where integer division truncates).

__floordiv__(self, other)
> Invoked on self // other for truncating (always) division.

__mod__(self, other)
> Invoked on self % other.

__divmod__(self, other)
> Invoked on divmod(self, other).

__pow__(self, other [, modulo])
> Invoked on pow(self, other [, modulo]) and self ** other.

__lshift__(self, other)
> Invoked on self << other.

__rshift__(self, other)
> Invoked on self >> other.

__and__(self, other)
> Invoked on self & other.

__xor__(self, other)
> Invoked on self ^ other.

__or__(self, other)
> Invoked on self | other.

Right-side binary methods

```
__radd__(self, other),
__rsub__(self, other),
__rmul__(self, other),
__rtruediv__(self, other),
__rfloordiv__(self, other),
__rmod__(self, other),
__rdivmod__(self, other),
__rpow__(self, other),
__rlshift__(self, other),
__rrshift__(self, other),
__rand__(self, other),
__rxor__(self, other),
__ror__(self, other)
```

These are right-side counterparts to the binary operators of the prior section. Binary operator methods have a right-side variant that starts with an **r** prefix (e.g., __add__ and __radd__). Right-side variants have the same argument lists, but self is on the right side of the operator. For instance, self + other calls self.__add__(other), but other + self invokes self.__radd__(other).

The **r** right-side method is called only when the instance is on the right and the left operand is not an instance of a class that implements the operation:

> instance + noninstance runs __add__
> instance + instance runs __add__
> noninstance + instance runs __radd__

If two different class instances that overload the operation appear, the class on the left is preferred. __radd__ often converts or swaps order and re-adds to trigger __add__.

Augmented binary methods

```
__iadd__(self, other),
__isub__(self, other),
__imul__(self, other),
__itruediv__(self, other),
__ifloordiv__(self, other),
__imod__(self, other),
__ipow__(self, other[, modulo]),
__ilshift__(self, other),
__irshift__(self, other),
__iand__(self, other),
__ixor__(self, other),
__ior__(self, other)
```

> These are augmented assignment (in-place) methods. Respectively, they are called for the following assignment statement formats: +=, -=, *=, /=, //=, %=, **=, <<=, >>=, &=, ^=, and |=. These methods should attempt to do the operation in-place (modifying self) and return the result (which can be self). If a method is not defined, then the augmented operation falls back on the normal methods. To evaluate X += Y, where X is an instance of a class that has an __iadd__, x.__iadd__(y) is called. Otherwise, __add__ and __radd__ are considered.

For Numbers (Other Operations)

```
__neg__(self)
```
> Invoked on -self.

```
__pos__(self)
```
> Invoked on +self.

```
__abs__(self)
```
> Invoked on abs(self).

```
__invert__(self)
```
> Invoked on ~self.

__complex__(self)
  Invoked on `complex(self)`.

__int__(self)
  Invoked on `int(self)`.

__float__(self)
  Invoked on `float(self)`.

__round__(self [, n])
  Invoked on `round(self [, n])`. New in Python 3.0.

__index__(self)
  Called to implement `operator.index()`. Also called in other contexts where Python requires an integer object. This includes instance appearances as indexes, as slice bounds, and as arguments to the built-in `bin()`, `hex()`, and `oct()` functions. Must return an integer.

  Similar in Python 3.0 and 2.6, but not called for `hex()` and `oct()` in 2.6 (these require `__hex__` and `__oct__` methods in 2.6). In Python 3.0, `__index__` subsumes and replaces the `__oct__` and `__hex__` methods of Python 2.X, and the returned integer is formatted automatically.

For Descriptors

The following methods apply only when an instance of a class defining the method (a descriptor class) is assigned to a class attribute of another class (known as the owner class). These methods are invoked for access to the attribute in the owner class whose name is assigned to the descriptor class instance.

__get__(self, instance, owner)
  Called to get the attribute of the owner class or of an instance of that class. `owner` is always the owner class; `instance` is the instance the attribute was accessed through, or `None` when the attribute is accessed through the owner class directly. Return the attribute value or raise `AttributeError`.

`__set__(self, instance, value)`
> Called to set the attribute on an instance of the owner class to a new value.

`__delete__(self, instance)`
> Called to delete the attribute on an instance of the owner class.

For Context Managers

The following methods implement the context manager protocol, used by the `with` statement (see "The with Statement" on page 80).

`__enter__(self)`
> Enter the runtime context related to this object. The `with` statement assigns this method's return value to the target specified in the `as` clause of the statement (if any).

`__exit__(self, exc_type, exc_value, traceback)`
> Exit the runtime context related to this object. The parameters describe the exception that caused the context to be exited. If the context exited without an exception, all three arguments are None. Return a true value to prevent a raised exception from being propagated by the caller.

Python 2.X Operator Overloading Methods

Methods in Python 3.0 only

The following methods are supported in Python 3.0 but not Python 2.X:

- `__bool__` (use method name `__nonzero__` in Python 2.X, or `__len__`)
- `__next__` (use method name next in Python 2.X)
- `__truediv__` (available in Python 2.X only if true division is enabled)
- `__dir__`

- `__round__`
- `__index__` for oct(), hex() (use `__oct__`, `__hex__` in Python 2.X)

Methods in Python 2.X only

The following methods are supported in Python 2.X but not Python 3.0:

`__cmp__(self, other)` *(and `__rcmp__`)*
> Invoked on `self > x`, `x == self`, `cmp(self, x)`, etc. This method is called for all comparisons for which no more specific method (such as `__lt__`) is defined or inherited. It returns -1, 0, or 1 for `self` less than, equal to, or greater than `other`. If no rich comparison or `__cmp__` methods are defined, class instances compare by their identity (address in memory). The `__rcmp__` right-side method is no longer supported as of version 2.1.
>
> In Python 3.0, use the more specific comparison methods described earlier: `__lt__`, `__ge__`, `__eq__`, etc. Use `__lt__` for sorting in Python 3.0.

`__nonzero__(self)`
> Invoked on truth-value (otherwise, uses `__len__` if defined).
>
> In Python 3.0, this method is renamed `__bool__`.

`__getslice__(self, low, high)`
> Invoked on `self[low:high]` for sequence slicing. If no `__getslice__` is found, and for extended three-item slices, a *slice object* is created and passed to the `__getitem__` method instead.
>
> In Python 2.X, this and the next two methods are considered deprecated but are still supported—they are called for slice expressions if defined, in preference to their item-based counterparts. In Python 3.0, these three methods are removed entirely—slices always invoke `__getitem__`, `__setitem__`, or `__delitem__` instead, with a slice object as

its argument. See slice() in "Built-in Functions" on page 102.

__setslice__(self, low, high, seq)
Invoked on self[low:high]=seq for sequence slice assignment.

__delslice__(self, low, high)
Invoked on del self[low:high] for sequence slice deletion.

__div__(self, other) (and __rdiv__, __idiv__)
Invoked on self / other, unless true division is enable with from (in which case __truediv__ is used). In Python 3.0, these are always subsumed by __truediv__, __rtruediv__, and __itruediv__ because / is always true division.

__long__(self)
Invoked on long(self). In Python 3.0, the int type subsumes the long type completely.

__oct__(self)
Invoked on oct(self). This method returns an octal string representation. In Python 3.0, return an integer for __index__() instead.

__hex__(self)
Invoked on hex(self). This method returns a hex string representation. In Python 3.0, return an integer for __index__() instead.

__coerce__(self, other)
Invoked on the mixed-mode arithmetic expression, coerce(). This method returns a tuple of (self, other) converted to a common type. If __coerce__ is defined, it is generally called before any real operator methods are tried (e.g., before __add__). It should return a tuple containing operands converted to a common type (or None if it can't convert). See the Python Language Reference (http://www.python.org/doc/) for more on coercion rules.

__metaclass__

    Class attribute assigned to class's metaclass. In Python 3.0, use metaclass=M keyword argument syntax in the class header line.

Built-in Functions

All built-in names (functions, exceptions, and so on) exist in the implied outer built-in scope, which corresponds to the builtins module (named __builtin__ in Python 2). Because this scope is always searched last on name lookups, these functions are always available in programs without imports. However, their names are not reserved words and might be hidden by assignments to the same name in global or local scopes.

abs(N)

    Returns the absolute value of a number N.

all(iterable)

    Returns True only if all elements of the iterable are true.

any(iterable)

    Returns True only if any element of the iterable is true.

ascii(object)

    Like repr(), returns a string containing a printable representation of an object, but escapes the non-ASCII characters in the repr() result string using \x, \u, or \U escapes. This result is similar to that returned by repr() in Python 2.X.

bin(N)

    Convert an integer number to a binary (base 2) digits string. The result is a valid Python expression. If argument N is not a Python int object, it must define an __index__() method that returns an integer. See also int(x, 2) to convert from binary, 0bNNN binary literals, and the b type code in str.format().

bool([x])

    Converts a value to a Boolean, using the standard truth testing procedure. If x is false or omitted, this returns

False; otherwise, it returns True. bool is also a class, which is a subclass of int. The class bool cannot be subclassed further. Its only instances are False and True.

bytearray([arg [, encoding [, errors]]])

Returns a new array of bytes. The bytearray type is a mutable sequence of small integers in the range 0...255, which prints as ASCII text when possible. It is essentially a mutable variant of bytes, which supports most operations of mutable sequences, as well as most methods of the str string type. arg may be a str string with encoding name (and optionally errors) as in str(); an integer size to initialize an array of NULL bytes; an iterable of small integers used to initialize the array such as a bytes string or another bytearray; an object conforming to the memory-view (previously known as buffer) interface used to initialize the array; or absent, to create a zero-length array.

bytes([arg [, encoding [, errors]]])

Returns a new bytes object, which is an immutable sequence of integers in the range 0...255. bytes is an immutable version of bytearray. It has the same nonmutating string methods and sequence operations. It is commonly used to represent 8-bit byte strings of binary data. Constructor arguments are interpreted as for bytearray(). bytes objects may also be created with the b'ccc' literal.

chr(I)

Returns a one-character string whose Unicode codepoint is integer I. This is the inverse of ord() (e.g., chr(97) is 'a' and ord('a') is 97).

classmethod(function)

Returns a class method for a function. A class method receives the class as an implicit first argument, just like an instance method receives the instance. Use the @classmethod function decorator in version 2.4 and later (see the section "The def Statement" on page 64).

`compile(string, filename, kind [, flags[, dont_inherit]])`

Compiles **string** into a code object. **string** is a Python string containing Python program code. **filename** is a string used in error messages (and is usually the name of the file from which the code was read, or `<string>` if typed interactively). **kind** can be `'exec'` if **string** contains statements; `'eval'` if **string** is an expression; or `'single'`, which prints the output of an expression statement that evaluates to something other than **None**. The resulting code object can be executed with **exec()** or **eval()** built-in function calls. The optional last two arguments control which future statements affect the string's compilation; if absent, the string is compiled with the future statements in effect at the place of the **compile()** call (see Python manuals for more details).

`complex([real [, imag]])`

Builds a complex number object (this can also be done using the **J** or **j** suffix: `real+imagJ`). **imag** defaults to 0. If both arguments are omitted, returns `0j`.

`delattr(object, name)`

Deletes the attribute named **name** (a string) from **object**. It is similar to `del obj.name`, but **name** is a string, not a variable (e.g., `delattr(a,'b')` is like `del a.b`).

`dict([mapping | iterable | keywords])`

Returns a new dictionary initialized from a mapping; a sequence (or other iterable) of key/value pairs; or a set of keyword arguments. If no argument is given, it returns an empty dictionary. This is a subclassable type class name.

`dir([object])`

If no arguments, this returns the list of names in the current local scope (namespace). With any object with attributes as an argument, it returns the list of attribute names associated with that **object**. It works on modules, classes, and class instances, as well as built-in objects with attributes (lists, dictionaries, etc.). Its result includes inherited attributes, and is sorted. Use `__dict__` attributes

for simple attribute lists of a single object (and possibly
__slots__ for some classes).

`divmod(X, Y)`

Returns a tuple of (X / Y, X % Y).

`enumerate(iterable, start=0)`

Returns an iterable enumerate object. iterable must be a
sequence, an iterator, or some other object that supports
iteration. The __next__() method of the iterator returned
by enumerate() returns a tuple containing a count (from
start, or zero by default) and the corresponding value
obtained from iterating over iterable. This call is useful
for obtaining an indexed series when both positions and
items are required in for loops: (0, seq[0]), (1,
seq[1]), (2, seq[2]).... Available in version 2.3 and later.

`eval(expr [, globals [, locals]])`

Evaluates expr, which is assumed to be either a Python
string containing a Python expression or a compiled code
object. expr is evaluated in the namespace scopes of the
eval call itself, unless the globals and/or locals namespace dictionary arguments are passed. locals defaults to
globals if only globals is passed. It returns an expr result.
Also see the compile function discussed earlier in this section, and the exec() built-in for dynamically running
statements.

`exec(stmts [, globals [, locals]])`

Evaluates stmts, which is assumed to be either a Python
string containing Python statements or a compiled code
object. If stmts is a string, the string is parsed as a suite of
Python statements, which is then executed unless a syntax
error occurs. If it is a code object, it is simply executed.
globals and locals work the same as in eval(), and
compile() may be used to precompile to code objects. This
is available as a statement form in Python 2.X (see "Specific Statements" on page 56).

`filter(function, iterable)`

> Returns those elements of `iterable` for which `function` returns `true`. `function` takes one parameter. If `function` is `None`, this returns all the true items.
>
> In Python 2.6 this call returns a list. In Python 3.0, it returns an iterable object that generates values on demand and can be traversed only once (wrap in a `list()` call to force results generation if required).

`float([X])`

> Converts a number or a string `X` to a floating-point number (or `0.0` if no argument is passed). This is a subclassable type class name.

`format(value [, formatspec])`

> Converts an object `value` to a formatted representation, as controlled by string `formatspec`. The interpretation of `formatspec` depends on the type of the `value` argument (a standard formatting syntax is used by most built-in types, described for the string formatting method earlier in this book). `format(value, formatspec)` calls `value.__format__(formatspec)`, and is a base operation of the `str.format` method (e.g., `format(1.3333, '.2f')` is equivalent to `'{0:.2f}'.format(1.3333)`).

`frozenset([iterable])`

> Returns a *frozen set* object whose elements are taken from iterable. Frozen sets are immutable sets that have no update methods, and may be nested in other sets.

`getattr(object, name [, default])`

> Returns the value of attribute `name` (a string) from `object`. It is similar to `object.name`, but `name` is a string, not a variable (e.g., `getattr(a,'b')` is like `a.b`). If the named attribute does not exist, `default` is returned if provided; otherwise, `AttributeError` is raised.

`globals()`

> Returns a dictionary containing the caller's global variables (e.g., the enclosing module's names).

`hasattr(object, name)`

> Returns `true` if `object` has an attribute called `name` (a string); false otherwise.

`hash(object)`

> Returns the hash value of `object` (if it has one). Hash values are integers used to quickly compare dictionary keys during a dictionary lookup.

`help([object])`

> Invokes the built-in help system. (This function is intended for interactive use.) If no argument is given, an interactive help session starts in the interpreter console. If the argument is a string, it is looked up as the name of a module, function, class, method, keyword, or documentation topic, and its help text is displayed. If the argument is any other kind of object, help for that object is generated.

`hex(N)`

> Converts an integer number `N` to a hexadecimal (base 16) digits string. If argument `N` is not a Python `int` object, it must define an `__index__()` method that returns an integer.

`id(object)`

> Returns the unique identity integer of `object` (i.e., its address in memory).

`__import__(name`
`[, globals [, locals [, fromlist [, level] ]]])`

> Imports and returns a module, given its `name` as a string at runtime (e.g., `mod = __import__("mymod")`). This call is generally faster than constructing and executing an `import` statement string with `exec()`. This function is called by `import` and `from` statements internally and can be overridden to customize import operations. All arguments but the first have advanced roles (see the Python Library Reference). See also the `imp` standard library module for related tools.

`input([prompt])`

>   Prints a `prompt` string if given, then reads a line from the *stdin* input stream (`sys.stdin`) and returns it as a string. It strips the trailing `\n` at the end of the line and raises `EOFError` at the end of the *stdin* stream. On platforms where GNU `readline` is supported, `input()` uses it. In Python 2.X, this function is named `raw_input()`.

`int([number | string [, base]])`

>   Converts a number or string to a plain integer. Conversion of floating-point numbers to integers truncates toward 0. `base` can be passed only if the first argument is a string, and defaults to 10. If `base` is passed as 0, the base is determined by the string's contents; otherwise, the value passed for `base` is used for the base of the conversion of the string. `base` may be 0, and 2...36. The string may be preceded by a sign and surrounded by whitespace. If no arguments, returns 0. This is a subclassable type class name.

`isinstance(object, classinfo)`

>   Returns `true` if `object` is an instance of `classinfo`, or an instance of any subclass thereof. `classinfo` can also be a tuple of classes and/or types. In Python 3.0, types are classes, so there is no special case for types. In Python 2.X, the second argument can also be a type object, making this function useful as an alternative type-testing tool (`isinstance(X, Type)` versus `type(X) is Type`).

`issubclass(class1, class2)`

>   Returns `true` if `class1` is derived from `class2`. `class2` can also be a tuple of classes.

`iter(object [, sentinel])`

>   Returns an iterator object that can be used to step through items in `object`. Iterator objects returned have a `__next__()` method that returns the next item or raises `StopIteration` to end the progression. All iteration contexts in Python use this protocol to advance, if supported by `object`. The `next(I)` built-in function also calls `I.__next__()` automatically. If one argument, `object` is

assumed to provide its own iterator or be a sequence; if two arguments, `object` is a callable that is called until it returns `sentinel`. The `iter()` call can be overloaded in classes with `__iter__`.

In Python 2.X, iterable objects have a method named `next()` instead of `__next__()`. For forward compatibility, the `next()` built-in function is available in 2.6 and calls `I.next()` instead of `I.__next__()` (prior to 2.6, `I.next()` may be called manually instead).

`len(object)`

> Returns the number of items (length) in a collection `object`, which may be a sequence or mapping.

`list([iterable])`

> Returns a new list containing all the items in any `iterable` object. If `iterable` is already a list, it returns a copy of it. If no arguments, returns a new empty list. This is a subclassable type class name.

`locals()`

> Returns a dictionary containing the local variables of the caller (with one *key:value* entry per local).

`map(function, iterable [, iterable]*)`

> Applies `function` to each item of any sequence or other iterable `iterable`, and returns the individual results. For example, `map(abs, (1, -2))` returns 1 and 2. If additional iterable arguments are passed, `function` must take that many arguments, and it is passed one item from each iterable on every call; iteration stops at the end of the shortest iterable.
>
> In Python 2.6, this returns a list of the individual call results. In Python 3.0, it instead returns an iterable object that generates results on demand and can be traversed only once (wrap it in a `list()` call to force results generation if required). Also in Python 2.X (but not Python 3), if `function` is `None`, `map` collects all the items into a result list; if sequences differ in length, all are padded to the

length of the longest, with `None`s. Similar utility is available in Python 3.0 in module `itertools`.

`max(iterable [, arg]* [, key])`

> With a single argument `iterable`, returns the largest item of a nonempty iterable (e.g., string, tuple, and list). With more than one argument, it returns the largest of all the arguments. The optional keyword-only `key` argument specifies a one-argument value transform function like that used for `list.sort()` and `sorted()`.

`memoryview(object)`

> Returns a memory view object created from the given argument. Memory views allow Python code to access the internal data of an object that supports the protocol without copying the object. Memory can be interpreted as simple bytes or more complex data structures. Built-in objects that support the memory-view protocol include `bytes` and `bytearray`. See Python manuals; memory views are largely a replacement for the Python 2.X *buffer* protocol and built-in function.

`min(iterable [, arg]* [, key])`

> With a single argument `iterable`, returns the smallest item of a nonempty iterable (e.g., string, tuple, list). With more than one argument, it returns the smallest of all the arguments. The key argument is as in `max()`.

`next(iterator [, default])`

> Retrieves the next item from the `iterator` by calling its `__next__()` method. If the `iterator` is exhausted, `default` is returned if given; otherwise, `StopIteration` is raised.

> This is available in Python 2.6 for forward compatibility, but it calls `iterator.next()` instead of `iterator.__next__()`. In Python 2.X prior to 2.6, this call is missing; use `iterator.next()` manually instead.

`object()`

> Returns a new featureless object. `object` is a base for all new style classes, which includes classes explicitly derived from `object` in Python 2.X, and all classes in Python 3.0.

---

oct(N)

>   Converts a number **N** to an octal (base 8) digits string. If
>   argument **N** is not a Python **int** object, it must define a
>   __index__() method that returns an integer.

open(…)

```
open(file [, mode='r'
    [, buffering=None
    [, encoding=None        # text mode only
    [, errors=None          # text mode only
    [, newline=None         # text mode only
    [, closefd=True] ]]]]]) # descriptors only
```

Returns a new file object connected to the external file named
by **file**, or raises **IOError** if the open fails. **file** is usually a string
or bytes object giving the name (and the path if the file isn't in
the current working directory) of the file to be opened. **file**
may also be an integer file descriptor of the file to be wrapped.
If a file descriptor is given, it is closed when the returned I/O
object is closed, unless **closefd** is set to **False**. All options may
be passed as keyword arguments.

mode is an optional string that specifies the mode in which the
file is opened. It defaults to **'r'**, which means open for reading
in text mode. Other common values are **'w'** for writing (truncating the file if it already exists), and **'a'** for appending. In text
mode, if **encoding** is not specified, the encoding used is platform dependent, and newlines are translated to and from
'\n' by default. For reading and writing raw bytes, use binary
modes **'rb'**, **'wb'**, or **'ab'**, and leave **encoding** unspecified.

Available modes that may be combined: **'r'** for read (default);
'w' for write, truncating the file first; **'a'** for write, appending
to the end of the file if it exists; **'b'** for binary mode; **'t'** for
text mode (default); **'+'** to open a disk file for updating (reading
and writing); **'U'** for universal newline mode (for backward
compatibility, not needed for new code). The default **'r'** mode
is the same as **'rt'** (open for reading text). For binary random
access, the mode **'w+b'** opens and truncates the file to 0 bytes,
while **'r+b'** opens the file without truncation.

Python distinguishes between files opened in binary and text modes, even when the underlying operating system does not.‖

- For *input*, files opened in binary mode (by appending `'b'` to `mode`) return contents as `bytes` objects without any Unicode decoding or line-end translations. In text mode (the default, or when `'t'` is appended to `mode`), the contents of the file are returned as `str` strings after the bytes are decoded using either an explicitly passed `encoding` name or a platform-dependent default, and line-ends are translated per `newline`.

- For *output*, binary mode expects a `bytes` or `bytearray` and writes it unchanged. Text mode expects a `str`, and encodes it per `encoding` and applies line-end translations per `newline` before writing.

`buffering` is an optional integer used to set buffering policy. By default, full buffering is on. Pass 0 to switch buffering off (allowed in binary mode only); 1 to set line buffering; and an integer > 1 for full buffering. Buffered data transfers might not be immediately fulfilled (use `file.flush` to force).

`encoding` is the name of the encoding used to decode or encode a text file's content on transfers. This should be used in text mode only. The default encoding is platform dependent, but any encoding supported by Python can be passed. See the `codecs` module for the list of supported encodings.

`errors` is an optional string that specifies how encoding errors are to be handled. This should be used in text mode only. Pass `'strict'` to raise a `ValueError` exception if there is an encoding error (the default of `None` has the same effect), or pass `'ignore'` to ignore errors. Ignoring encoding errors can lead to

---

‖ In fact, because file mode implies both configuration options and string data types, it's probably best to think of open() in terms of two distinct flavors—text and binary, as specified in the mode string. Python developers chose to overload a single function to support the two file types, with mode-specific arguments and differing content types, rather than provide two separate open functions and file object types.

data loss. See `codecs.register()` for a list of the permitted values.

`newline` controls how universal newlines work, and applies to text mode only. It can be `None` (the default), `''`, `'\n'`, `'\r'`, and `'\r\n'`.

- On *input*, if `newline` is `None`, universal newlines mode is enabled: lines may end in `'\n'`, `'\r'`, or `'\r\n'`, and all these are translated to `'\n'` before being returned to the caller. If `newline` is `''`, universal newline mode is enabled, but line endings are returned to the caller untranslated. If it has any of the other legal values, input lines are only terminated by the given string, and the line ending is returned to the caller untranslated.

- On *output*, if `newline` is `None`, any `'\n'` characters written are translated to the system default line separator, `os.linesep`. If `newline` is `''`, no translation takes place. If it is any of the other legal values, any `'\n'` characters written are translated to the given string.

If `closefd` is `False`, the underlying file descriptor will be kept open when the file is closed. This does not work when a file name is given as a string and must be `True` (the default) in that case.

`ord(C)`
    Returns an integer codepoint value of a one-character string `C`. For ASCII characters, this is the 7-bit ASCII code of `C`; for wider Unicode, this is the Unicode code point of a one-character Unicode string.

`pow(X, Y [, Z])`
    Returns `X` to power `Y` [modulo `Z`]. It is similar to the `**` expression operator.

`print([object,...]`
`[, sep=' '] [, end='\n'] [, file=sys.stdout])`
    Prints `object`(s) to the stream `file`, separated by `sep` and followed by `end`. `sep`, `end`, and `file`, if present, must be given as keyword arguments, and default as shown.

All nonkeyword arguments are converted to strings, like `str()` does, and written to the stream. Both `sep` and `end` must either be strings, or `None` (meaning use their default values). If no `object` is given, `end` is written. `file` must be an object with a `write(string)` method, but need not be an actual file; if it is not passed or is `None`, `sys.stdout` will be used. Print functionality is available as a statement form in Python 2.X (see "Specific Statements" on page 56).

`property([fget[, fset[, fdel[, doc]]]])`

Returns a property attribute for new-style classes (classes that derive from `object`). `fget` is a function for getting an attribute value, `fset` is a function for setting, and `fdel` is a function for deleting. This call may be used as a function decorator itself, and returns an object with methods `getter`, `setter`, and `deleter`, which may also be used as decorators in this role (see "The def Statement" on page 64).

`range([start,] stop [, step])`

Returns successive integers between `start` and `stop`. With one argument, it returns integers from zero through `stop-1`. With two arguments, it returns integers from `start` through `stop-1`. With three arguments, it returns integers from `start` through `stop-1`, adding `step` to each predecessor in the result. `start`, `step` default to 0, 1. `range(0, 20, 2)` is a list of even integers from 0 through 18. This call is often used to generate offset lists or repeat counts in `for` loops.

In Python 2.6 this call returns a list. In Python 3.0, it returns an iterable object that generates values on demand and can be traversed multiple times (wrap in a `list()` call to force results generation if required).

`repr(object)`

Returns a string containing a printable and potentially parseable as-code representation of any `object`. In Python 2.X (but not Python 3.0) this is equivalent to `` `object` `` (back quotes expression).

`reversed(seq)`

>   Returns a reverse iterator. `seq` must be an object that has a `__reversed__()` method or supports the sequence protocol (the `__len__()` method and the `__getitem__()` method with integer arguments starting at 0).

`round(X [, N])`

>   Returns the floating-point value `X` rounded to `N` digits after the decimal point. `N` defaults to zero, and may be negative to denote digits to the left of the decimal point. The return value is an integer if called with one argument, otherwise of the same type as `X`. In Python 2.X only, the result is always a floating-point. In Python 3.0 only, calls `X.__round__()`.

`set([iterable])`

>   Returns a set whose elements are taken from `iterable`. The elements must be immutable. To represent sets of sets, the nested sets should be `frozenset` objects. If `iterable` is not specified, this returns a new empty set. Available since version 2.4. See also the section "Sets" on page 49, and the {...} set literal in Python 3.0.

`setattr(object, name, value)`

>   Assigns `value` to the attribute `name` (a string) in `object`. Like `object.name = value`, but `name` is a runtime string, not a variable name taken literally (e.g., `setattr(a,'b',c)` is equivalent to `a.b=c`).

`slice([start ,] stop [, step])`

>   Returns a slice object representing a range, with read-only attributes `start`, `stop`, and `step`, any of which can be `None`. Arguments are the same as for `range`. Slice objects may be used in place of `i:j:k` slice notation (e.g., `X[i:j]` is equivalent to `X[slice(i, j)]`).

`sorted(iterable, key=None, reverse=False)`

>   Returns a new sorted list from the items in `iterable`. The optional keyword arguments `key` and `reverse` have the same meaning as those for the `list.sort()` method described earlier; `key` is a one-argument value transform function. This works on any iterable and returns a new

object instead of changing a list in-place, and is thus useful in **for** loops to avoid splitting sort calls out to separate statements due to **None** returns. Available in version 2.4 and later.

In Python 2.X, this has call signature `sorted(iterable, cmp=None, key=None, reverse=False)`, where optional arguments `cmp`, `key`, and `reverse` have the same meaning as those for the Python 2.X `list.sort()` method described earlier in this book.

`staticmethod(function)`

Returns a static method for **function**. A static method does not receive an implicit first argument, and so is useful for processing class attributes that span instances. Use the `@staticmethod` function decorator in version 2.4 and later (see the section "The def Statement" on page 64).

`str([object [, encoding [, errors]]])`

Returns a "user-friendly" and printable string version of an object. This is also a subclassable type name. Operates in one of the following modes:

- When only **object** is given, this returns its nicely printable representation. For strings, this is the string itself. The difference with `repr(object)` is that `str(object)` does not always attempt to return a string that is acceptable to `eval()`; its goal is to return a printable string. With no arguments, this returns the empty string.

- If **encoding** and/or **errors** are passed, this will decode the object, which can either be a byte string or a character buffer, using the codec for **encoding**. The **encoding** parameter is a string giving the name of an encoding; if the encoding is not known, **LookupError** is raised. Error handling is done according to **errors**; if errors is `'strict'` (the default), a **ValueError** is raised for encoding errors, while a value of `'ignore'` causes errors to be silently ignored, and a value of `'replace'` causes the official Unicode replacement character, U +FFFD, to be used to replace input characters that cannot be decoded. See also the `codecs` module, and the similar `bytes.decode()` method (`b'a\xe4'.decode('latin-1')` is equivalent to `str(b'a\xe4', 'latin-1')`).

In Python 2.X, this call has simpler signature `str([object])`, and returns a string containing the printable representation of `object` (the first usage mode in Python 3.0).

`sum(iterable [, start])`

Sums `start` and the items of an iterable, from left to right, and returns the total. `start` defaults to 0. The iterable's items are normally numbers and are not allowed to be strings (to concatenate an iterable of strings, use `''.join(iterable)`).

`super([type [, object-or-type]])`

Returns the superclass of `type`. If the second argument is omitted, the super object returned is unbound. If the second argument is an object, `isinstance(obj, type)` must be true. If the second argument is a type, `issubclass(type2, type)` must be true. Calling `super()` without arguments is equivalent to `super(this_class, first_arg)`. In a single-inheritance class hierarchy, this call can be used to refer to parent classes without naming them explicitly. This call can also be used to implement cooperative multiple inheritance in a dynamic execution environment.

This works only for new-style classes in Python 2.X (where `type` is not optional), and for all classes in Python 3.0.

`tuple([iterable])`

Returns a new tuple with the same elements as any `iterable` passed in. If `iterable` is already a tuple, it is returned directly (not a copy). If no argument, returns a new empty tuple. This is also a subclassable type class name.

`type(object | (name, bases, dict))`

This call is used in two different modes, determined by call pattern:

- With one argument, returns a type object representing the type of `object`. Useful for type-testing in `if` statements (e.g., `type(X)==type([])`), as well as dictionary keys. See also module `types` for preset type objects that are not built-in names, and `isinstance()` earlier in this section. Due to the recent merging of types and classes, `type(object)` is generally the same as `object.__class__`. In Python 2.X, the `types` module also includes built-in types.

- With three arguments, serves as a constructor, returning a new type object. This is a dynamic form of the `class` statement. The `name` string is the class name and becomes the `__name__` attribute; the `bases` tuple itemizes the base classes and becomes the `__bases__` attribute; and the `dict` dictionary is the namespace containing definitions for class body and becomes the `__dict__` attribute. `class X(object): a = 1` is equivalent to `X = type('X', (object,), dict(a=1))`. This mapping is commonly used for metaclass construction.

`vars([object])`

Without arguments, returns a dictionary containing the current local scope's names. With a module, class, or class instance object as an argument, it returns a dictionary corresponding to `object`'s attribute namespace (i.e., its `__dict__`). The result should not be modified. Useful for % string formatting.

`zip([iterable [, iterable]*])`

Returns a series of tuples, where each ith tuple contains the ith element from each of the argument iterables. For example, `zip('ab', 'cd')` returns `('a', 'c')` and `('b', 'd')`. At least one iterable is required, or the result is empty. The result series is truncated to the length of the shortest argument iterable. With a single iterable argument, it returns a series of one-tuples. May also be used to unzip zipped tuples: `X, Y = zip(*zip(T1, T2))`.

In Python 2.6, this returns a list. In Python 3.0, it returns an iterable object that generates values on demand and can be traversed only once (wrap in a `list()` call to force results generation if required). In Python 2.X (but not Python 3), when there are multiple argument iterables of the same length, `zip` is similar to `map` with a first argument of `None`.

Python 2.X Built-in Functions

The prior section's list applies to Python 3. Semantic differences between built-ins available in both Python 3.0 and 2.X are noted in the prior section.

Python 3.0 built-ins not supported by Python 2.6

Python 2.X does not have the following Python 3.0 built-in functions:

- `ascii()` (this works like Python 2's `repr()`)
- `exec()` (this is a statement form in Python 2.X with similar semantics)
- `memoryview()`
- `print()` (present in Python 2's `__builtin__` module, but not directly usable syntactically, as printing is a statement form and reserved word in Python 2.X)

Python 2.6 built-ins not supported by Python 3.0

Python 2.X has the following additional built-in functions, some of which are available in different forms in Python 3.0:

`apply(func, pargs [, kargs])`
> Calls any callable object `func` (a function, method, class, etc.), passing the positional arguments in tuple `pargs`, and the keyword arguments in dictionary `kargs`. It returns the `func` call result.
>
> In Python 3.0, this is removed. Use the argument-unpacking call syntax instead: `func(*pargs, **kargs)`. This form

is also preferred in Python 2.6 as it is more general and symmetric with function definitions.

`basestring()`

The baseclass for normal and Unicode strings (useful for **isinstance** tests).

In Python 3.0, the single **str** type represents all text (wide Unicode and other).

`buffer(object [, offset [, size]])`

Returns a new buffer object for a conforming **object** (see the Python Library Reference).

This call is removed in Python 3.0. The new **memory view()** built-in provides similar functionality.

`callable(object)`

Returns 1 if **object** is callable; otherwise, returns 0.

This call is removed in Python 3.0. Use **hasattr(f, '__call__')** instead.

`cmp(X, Y)`

Returns a negative integer, zero, or a positive integer to designate X < Y, X == Y, or X > Y, respectively.

In Python 3.0, this is removed, but may be simulated as: (X > Y) - (X < Y). However, most common **cmp()** use cases (comparison functions in sorts, and the __cmp__ method of classes) have also been removed in Python 3.0.

`coerce(X, Y)`

Returns a tuple containing the two numeric arguments X and Y converted to a common type.

This call is removed in Python 3.0 (its main use case was for Python 2.X classic classes).

`execfile(filename [, globals [, locals]])`

Like **eval**, but runs all the code in a file whose string name is passed in as **filename** (instead of an expression). Unlike imports, this does not create a new module object for the file. It returns **None**. Namespaces for code in **filename** are as for **eval**.

In Python 3.0, this may be simulated as: `exec(open(filename).read())`.

`file(filename [, mode[, bufsize]])`

An alias for the `open()` built-in function, and the subclassable class name of the built-in file type.

In Python 3.0, the name `file` is removed: use `open()` to create file objects, and `io` module classes to customize file operation.

`input([prompt])` (original form)

Prints `prompt`, if given. Then it reads an input line from the *stdin* stream (`sys.stdin`), evaluates it as Python code, and returns the result. It is like `eval(raw_input(prompt))`.

In Python 3.0, because `raw_input()` was renamed `input()`, the original Python 2.X `input()` is no longer available, but may be simulated as: `eval(input{prompt})`.

`intern(string)`

Enters `string` in the table of "interned strings" and returns the interned string. Interned strings are "immortals" and serve as a performance optimization (they can be compared by fast `is` identity, rather than `==` equality).

In Python 3.0, this call has been moved to `sys.intern()`. Import module `sys` to use it.

`long(X [, base])`

Converts a number or a string `X` to a long integer. `base` can be passed only if `X` is a string. If 0, the base is determined by the string contents; otherwise, it is used for the base of the conversion. It is a subclassable type class name.

In Python 3.0, the `int` integer type supports arbitrarily long precision, and so subsumes Python 2's `long` type. Use `int()` in Python 3.0.

`raw_input([prompt])`

This is the Python 2.X name of the Python 3.0 `input()` function described in the prior section.

In Python 3.0, use the `input()` built-in.

```
reduce(func, iterable [, init])
```
Applies the two-argument function `func` to successive items from `iterable`, so as to reduce the collection to a single value. If `init` is given, it is prepended to `iterable`.

In Python 3.0, this built-in is still available, as `functools.reduce()`. Import module `functools` to use it.

```
reload(module)
```
Reloads, re-parses, and re-executes an already imported `module` in the module's current namespace. Re-execution replaces prior values of the module's attributes in-place. `module` must reference an existing module object; it is not a new name or a string. This is useful in interactive mode if you want to reload a module after fixing it, without restarting Python. It returns the `module` object.

In Python 3.0, this built-in is still available as `imp.reload()`. Import module `imp` to use it.

```
unichr(i)
```
Returns the Unicode string of one character whose Unicode code is the integer `i` (e.g., `unichr(97)` returns the string `u'a'`). This is the inverse of `ord` for Unicode strings, and the Unicode version of `chr()`. The argument must be in range 0...65535 inclusive, or `ValueError` is raised.

In Python 3.0, normal strings represent Unicode characters: use the `chr()` call instead (e.g., `ord('\xe4')` is 228, and `chr(228)` and `chr(0xe4)` both return `'ä'`).

```
unicode(string [, encoding [, errors]])
```
Decodes `string` using the codec for `encoding`. Error handling is done according to `errors`. The default behavior is to decode UTF-8 in strict mode, meaning that encoding errors raise `ValueError`. See also the `codecs` module in the Python Library Reference.

In Python 3.0, there is no separate type for Unicode—the `str` type represents all text (wide Unicode and other), and the `bytes` type represents 8-bit byte binary data. Use normal `str` strings for Unicode text; `bytes.decode()` or `str()` to decode from raw bytes to Unicode according to an encoding; and normal file objects to process Unicode text files.

xrange([start,] stop [, step])

Like range, but doesn't actually store the entire list all at once (rather, it generates one integer at a time). This is useful in for loops when there is a big range and little memory. It optimizes space, but generally has no speed benefit.

In Python 3.0, the original range() function is changed to return an iterable instead of producing a result list in memory, and thus subsumes Python 2's xrange(). Use range() in Python 3.0.

In addition, the file open call has changed radically enough in Python 3.0 that individual mention of Python 2's variant is warranted (in Python 2.X, codecs.open has many of the features in Python 3's open):

open(filename [, mode, [bufsize]])

Returns a new file object connected to the external file named filename (a string), or raises IOError if the open fails. The file name is mapped to the current working directory, unless it includes a directory path prefix. The first two arguments are generally the same as those for C's fopen function, and the file is managed by the stdio system. With open(), file data is always represented as a normal str string in your script, containing bytes from the file (codecs.open() interprets file content as encoded Unicode text, represented as unicode objects).

mode defaults to 'r' if omitted, but can be 'r' for input; 'w' for output (truncating the file first); 'a' for append; and 'rb', 'wb', or 'ab' for binary files (to suppress line-end conversions to and from \n). On most systems, most of these can also have a + appended to open in input/output updates mode (e.g., 'r+' to read/write, and 'w+' to read/write but initialize the file to empty).

bufsize defaults to an implementation-dependent value, but can be 0 for unbuffered, 1 for line-buffered, negative for system-default, or a given specific size. Buffered data transfers might not be immediately fulfilled (use file **flush** methods to force).

Built-in Exceptions

This section describes the exceptions that Python might raise during a program's execution. Beginning with Python 1.5, all built-in exceptions are class objects (prior to 1.5 they were strings). Built-in exceptions are provided in the built-in scope namespace. Many built-in exceptions have associated state information that provides exception details.

Superclasses (Categories)

The following exceptions are used only as superclasses for other exceptions.

BaseException

> The root superclass for all built-in exceptions. It is not meant to be directly inherited by user-defined classes; use **Exception** for this role instead. If **str()** is called on an instance of this class, the representation of the constructor argument(s) passed when creating the instance are returned (or the empty string if there were no such arguments). These instance constructor arguments are stored and made available in the instance's **args** attribute as a tuple. Subclasses inherit this protocol.

Exception

> The root superclass for all built-in and non-system-exiting exceptions. This is a direct subclass of **BaseException**.

> User-defined exceptions should inherit (be derived) from this class. This derivation is required for user-defined exceptions in Python 3.0; Python 2.6 requires this of new-style classes, but also allows standalone exception classes.

try statements that catch this exception will catch all but system exit events, because this class is superclass to all exceptions but **SystemExit**, **KeyboardInterrupt**, and **GeneratorExit** (these three derive directly from **BaseException** instead).

ArithmeticError

> Arithmetic error exceptions category: the superclass of **OverflowError**, **ZeroDivisionError**, and **FloatingPointError**, and a subclass of **Exception**.

LookupError

> Sequence and mapping index errors: the superclass for **IndexError** and **KeyError**, and a subclass of **Exception**.

EnvironmentError

> The category for exceptions that occur outside Python: the superclass for **IOError** and **OSError**, and a subclass of **Exception**. The raised instance includes informational attributes **errno** and **strerror** (and possible **filename** for exceptions involving file paths), which are also in **args**.

Specific Exceptions Raised

The following classes are exceptions that are actually raised. In addition, **NameError**, **RuntimeError**, **SyntaxError**, **ValueError**, and **Warning** are specific exceptions and superclasses to other built-in exceptions.

AssertionError

> Raised when an **assert** statement's test is false.

AttributeError

> Raised on attribute reference or assignment failure.

EOFError

> Raised when the immediate end-of-file is hit by **input()** (or **raw_input()** in Python 2). File read methods return an empty object at end of file instead.

FloatingPointError

> Raised on floating-point operation failure.

GeneratorExit

Raised when a generator's `close()` method is called. This directly inherits from `BaseException` instead of `Exception` since it is not an error.

IOError

Raised on I/O or file-related operation failures. Derived from `EnvironmentError` with state information described above.

ImportError

Raised when an `import` or `from` fails to find a module or attribute.

IndentationError

Raised when improper indentation is found in source code. Derived from `SyntaxError`.

IndexError

Raised on out-of-range sequence offsets (fetch or assign). Slice indexes are silently adjusted to fall in the allowed range; if an index is not an integer, `TypeError` is raised.

KeyError

Raised on references to nonexistent mapping keys (fetch). Assignment to a nonexistent key creates that key.

KeyboardInterrupt

Raised on user entry of the interrupt key (normally Ctrl-C or Delete). During execution, a check for interrupts is made regularly. This exception inherits directly from `Base Exception` to prevent it from being accidentally caught by code that catches `Exception` and thus prevents interpreter exit.

MemoryError

Raised on recoverable memory exhaustion. This causes a stack-trace to be displayed if a runaway program was its cause.

NameError

Raised on failures to find a local or global unqualified name.

NotImplementedError

Raised on failures to define expected protocols. Abstract class methods may raise this when they require a method to be redefined. Derived from `RuntimeError`. (This is not to be confused with `NotImplemented`, a special built-in object returned by some operator-overloading methods when operand types are not supported.)

OSError

Raised on `os` module errors (its `os.error` exception). Derived from `EnvironmentError` with state information described earlier.

OverflowError

Raised on excessively large arithmetic operations. This cannot occur for integers as they support arbitrary precision, and most floating-point operations are not checked either.

ReferenceError

Raised in conjunction with weak references. See the `weakref` module.

RuntimeError

A rarely used catch-all exception.

StopIteration

Raised on the end of values progression in iterator objects. Raised by the `next(X)` built-in and `X.__next__()` methods (`X.next()` in Python 2).

SyntaxError

Raised when parsers encounter a syntax error. This may occur during import operations, calls to `eval()` and `exec()`, and when reading code in a top-level script file or standard input. Instances of this class have attributes `filename`, `lineno`, `offset`, and `text` for access to details; `str()` of the exception instance returns only the message.

SystemError

Raised on interpreter internal errors that are not serious enough to shut down (these should be reported).

SystemExit

Raised on a call to `sys.exit(N)`. If not handled, the Python interpreter exits, and no stack traceback is printed. If the passed value is an integer, it specifies the system exit status (passed on to C's exit function); if it is `None`, the exit status is zero; if it has another type, the object's value is printed and the exit status is one. Derived directly from `BaseException` to prevent it from being accidentally caught by code that catches `Exception` and thus prevents interpreter exit.

`sys.exit()` raises this exception so that clean-up handlers (`finally` clauses of `try` statements) are executed, and so that a debugger can execute a script without losing control. The `os._exit()` function exits immediately when needed (e.g., in the child process after a call to `fork()`). Also see the `atexit` standard library module for exit function specification.

TabError

Raised when an improper mixture of spaces and tabs is found in source code. Derived from `IndentationError`.

TypeError

Raised when an operation or function is applied to an object of inappropriate type.

UnboundLocalError

Raised on references to local names that have not yet been assigned a value. Derived from `NameError`.

UnicodeError

Raised on Unicode-related encoding or decoding errors; a superclass category, and a subclass of `ValueError`.

UnicodeEncodeError,
UnicodeDecodeError,
UnicodeTranslateError

Raised on Unicode-related processing errors; subclasses of `UnicodeError`.

ValueError
> Raised when a built-in operation or function receives an argument that has the correct type but an inappropriate value, and the situation is not described by a more specific exception like IndexError.

WindowsError
> Raised on Windows-specific errors; a subclass of OSError.

ZeroDivisionError
> Raised on division or modulus operations with 0 on the right.

Warning Category Exceptions

The following exceptions are used as warning categories:

Warning
> The superclass for all of the following warning categories; it is a direct subclass of Exception.

UserWarning
> Warnings generated by user code.

DeprecationWarning
> Warnings about deprecated features.

PendingDeprecationWarning
> Warnings about features that will be deprecated in the future.

SyntaxWarning
> Warnings about dubious syntax.

RuntimeWarning
> Warnings about dubious runtime behavior.

FutureWarning
> Warnings about constructs that will change semantically in the future.

ImportWarning
> Warnings about probable mistakes in module imports.

`UnicodeWarning`
> Warnings related to Unicode.

`BytesWarning`
> Warnings related to `bytes` and buffer (memory-view) objects.

Warnings Framework

Warnings are issued when future language changes might break existing code in a future Python release—and in other contexts. Warnings may be configured to print messages, raise exceptions, or be ignored. The warnings framework can be used to issue warnings by calling the `warnings.warn` function:

```
warnings.warn("feature obsolete", DeprecationWarning)
```

In addition, you can add filters to disable certain warnings. You can apply a regular expression pattern to a message or module name to suppress warnings with varying degrees of generality. For example, you can suppress a warning about the use of the deprecated `regex` module by calling:

```
import warnings
warnings.filterwarnings(action = 'ignore',
                        message='.*regex module*',
                        category=DeprecationWarning,
                        module = '__main__')
```

This adds a filter that affects only warnings of the class `DeprecationWarning` triggered in the `__main__` module, applies a regular expression to match only the message that names the `regex` module being deprecated, and causes such warnings to be ignored. Warnings can also be printed only once, printed every time the offending code is executed, or turned into exceptions that will cause the program to stop (unless the exceptions are caught). See the `warnings` module documentation in version 2.1 and later for more information. See also the `-W` argument in the section "Command-Line Options" on page 4.

Python 2.X Built-in Exceptions

The set of available exceptions, as well as the shape of the exception class hierarchy, varies slightly in Python 2.6 from the 3.0 description of the prior section. For example, in Python 2.X:

- `Exception` is the topmost root class (not `BaseException`, which is absent in Python 2).

- `StandardError` is an additional `Exception` subclass, and is a root class above all built-in exceptions except `SystemExit`.

See Python 2.6 manuals for full details.

Built-in Attributes

Some objects export special attributes that are predefined by Python. The following is a partial list because many types have unique attributes all their own; see the entries for specific types in the Python Library Reference.#

`X.__dict__`
> Dictionary used to store object `X`'s writable attributes.

`I.__class__`
> Class object from which instance `I` was generated. In version 2.2 and later, this also applies to object types; most objects have a `__class__` attribute (e.g., `[].__class__` == `list` == `type([])`).

`C.__bases__`
> Tuple of class `C`'s base classes, as listed in `C`'s class statement header.

As of Python 2.1, you can also attach arbitrary user-defined attributes to *function* objects, simply by assigning them values. Python 2.X also supports special attributes `I.__methods__` and `I.__members__`: lists of method and data member names for instances of some built-in types. These are removed in Python 3; use the built-in `dir()` function.

`X.__name__`

    Object X's name as a string; for classes, the name in the statement header; for modules, the name as used in imports, or `"__main__"` for the module at the top level of a program (e.g., the main file run to launch a program).

Standard Library Modules

Standard library modules are always available but must be imported to be used in client modules. To access them, use one of these formats:

- `import module`, and fetch attribute names (`module.name`)
- `from module import name`, and use module names unqualified (`name`)
- `from module import *`, and use module names unqualified (`name`)

For instance, to use name `argv` in the `sys` module, either use `import sys` and name `sys.argv`, or use `from sys import argv` and name `argv`.

There are many standard library modules; the following sections are not necessarily exhaustive, and aim to document only commonly used names in commonly used modules. See Python's Library Reference for a more complete reference to standard library modules.

In all of the following module sections:

- Listed export names followed by parentheses are functions that must be called; others are simple attributes (i.e., variable names in modules).
- Module contents document the modules' state Python 3.0; see Python manuals for information on attributes unique to version 2 or 3.

The sys Module

The `sys` module contains interpreter-related exports. It also provides access to some environment components, such as the command line, standard streams, and so on.

`argv`

> Command-line argument strings list: `[command, arguments...]`. Like C's `argv` array.

`byteorder`

> Indicates the native byte-order (e.g., `big` for big-endian).

`builtin_module_names`

> Tuple of string names of C modules compiled into this Python interpreter.

`copyright`

> String containing the Python interpreter copyright.

`dllhandle`

> Python DLL integer handle; Windows only (see the Python Library Reference).

`displayhook(value)`

> Called by Python to display result values in interactive sessions; assign `sys.displayhook` to a one-argument function to customize output.

`excepthook(type, value, traceback)`

> Called by Python to display uncaught exception details to `stderr`; assign `sys.excepthook` to a three-argument function to customize exception displays.

`exc_info()`

> Returns tuple of three values describing the exception currently being handled `(type, value, traceback)`, where `type` is the exception class, `value` is the instance of the exception class raised, and `traceback` is an object that gives access to the runtime call stack as it existed when the exception occurred. Specific to current thread. Subsumes `exc_type`, `exc_value`, and `exc_traceback` in Python 1.5 and later (all three of which are removed completely in Python

3.0). See the **traceback** module in the Python Library Reference for processing traceback objects, and "The try Statement" on page 75 for more on exceptions.

exec_prefix

Assign to a string giving the site-specific directory prefix where the platform-dependent Python files are installed; defaults to */usr/local* or a build-time argument. Use this to locate shared library modules (in *<exec_prefix>/lib/ python<version>/lib-dynload*) and configuration files.

executable

String giving the full file pathname of the Python interpreter program running the caller.

exit([N])

Exits from a Python process with status **N** (default 0) by raising a **SystemExit** built-in exception (can be caught in a **try** statement and ignored). See also **SystemExit** (in "Built-in Exceptions" on page 124) and the **os._exit()** function (in "The os System Module" on page 141), which exits immediately without exception processing (useful in child processes after an **os.fork()**). Also see the **atexit** module for exit function specification.

getcheckinterval()

Returns the interpreter's "check interval"; see **setcheckinterval**, later in this list.

getdefaultencoding()

Returns the name of the current default string encoding used by the Unicode implementation.

getfilesystemencoding()

Returns the name of the encoding used to convert Unicode filenames into system file names, or **None** if the system default encoding is used.

getrefcount(object)

Returns **object**'s current reference count value (+1 for the call's argument).

`getrecursionlimit()`

Returns the maximum depth limit of the Python call stack; see also `setrecursionlimit`, later in this list.

`getsizeof(object [, default])`

Returns the size of an object in bytes. The object can be any type of object. All built-in objects return correct results, but third-party extension results are implementation specific. `default` provides a value that will be returned if the object type does not implement the size retrieval interface.

`_getframe([depth])`

Returns a frame object from the Python call stack (see the Python Library Reference).

`hexversion`

Python version number, encoded as a single integer (viewed best with the `hex()` built-in function). Increases with each new release.

`intern(string)`

Enters `string` in the table of "interned" strings and returns the interned string—the string itself or a copy. Interning strings provides a small performance improvement for dictionary lookup: if both the keys in a dictionary and the lookup key are interned, key comparisons (after hashing) can be done by comparing pointers instead of strings. Normally, names used in Python programs are automatically interned, and the dictionaries used to hold module, class, and instance attributes have interned keys.

`last_type`,
`last_value`,
`last_traceback`

Type, value, and traceback objects of last uncaught exception (mostly for postmortem debugging).

`maxsize`

An integer giving the maximum value a variable of type `Py_ssize_t` can take. It's usually $2**31 - 1$ on a 32-bit platform and $2**63 - 1$ on a 64-bit platform.

maxunicode

An integer giving the largest supported code point for a Unicode character. The value of this depends on the configuration option that specifies whether Unicode characters are stored as UCS-2 or UCS-4.

modules

Dictionary of modules that are already loaded; there is one `name:object` entry per module. Writable (for example, `del sys.modules['name']` forces a module to be reloaded on next import).

path

List of strings specifying module import search path. Initialized from **PYTHONPATH** shell variable, *.pth* path files, and any installation-dependent defaults. Writable (e.g., `sys.path.append('C:\\dir')` adds a directory to the search path within a script).

The first item, `path[0]`, is the directory containing the script that was used to invoke the Python interpreter. If the script directory is not available (e.g., if the interpreter is invoked interactively or if the script is read from standard input), `path[0]` is the empty string, which directs Python to search modules in the current working directory first. The script directory is inserted before the entries inserted from **PYTHONPATH**.

platform

String identifying the system on which Python is running: e.g., `'sunos5'`, `'darwin'`, `'linux2'`, `'win32'`, `'cygwin'`, `'PalmOS3'`. Useful for tests in platform-dependent code. Hint: `'win32'` means all current flavors of Windows, or test as `sys.platform[:3]=='win'` or `sys.platform.startswith('win')`.

prefix

Assign to a string giving the site-specific directory prefix, where platform-independent Python files are installed; defaults to */usr/local* or a build-time argument. Python library modules are installed in the directory *<prefix>/lib/*

---

python<version>; platform-independent header files are
stored in *<prefix>/include/python<version>*.

ps1

String specifying primary prompt in interactive mode; defaults to >>> unless assigned.

ps2

String specifying secondary prompt for compound statement continuations, in interactive mode; defaults to ...
unless assigned.

dont_write_bytecode

If this is true, Python won't try to write ".pyc" or ".pyo"
files on the import of source modules (see also "-B"
command-line option).

setcheckinterval(reps)

Call to set how often the interpreter checks for periodic
tasks (e.g., thread switches, signal handlers) to reps.
Measured in virtual machine instructions (default is 100).
In general, a Python statement translates to multiple virtual machine instructions. Lower values maximize thread
responsiveness but also maximize thread switch
overhead.

setdefaultencoding(name)

Call to set the current default string encoding used by the
Unicode implementation. Intended for use by the site
module and is available during start-up only.

setprofile(func)

Call to set the system profile function to func: the profiler's
"hook" (not run for each line). See the Python Library
Reference for details.

setrecursionlimit(depth)

Call to set maximum depth of the Python call stack to
depth. This limit prevents infinite recursion from causing
an overflow of the C stack and crashing Python. The default is 1,000 on Windows, but this may vary.

settrace(func)
> Call to set the system trace function to func: the program location or state change callback "hook" used by debuggers, etc. See the Python Library Reference for details.

stdin
> Standard input stream: a preopened file object. Can be assigned to any object with read methods to reset input within a script (e.g., sys.stdin=MyObj()). Used for interpreter input, including the input() built-in function (and raw_input() in Python 2).

stdout
> Standard output stream: a preopened file object. Can be assigned to any object with write methods to reset output within a script (e.g., sys.stdout=open('log', 'a')). Used for some prompts and the print() built-in function (and print statement in Python 2).

stderr
> Standard error stream: a preopened file object. Can be assigned to any object with write methods to reset stderr within a script (e.g., sys.stderr=wrappedsocket). Used for interpreter prompts/errors.

__stdin__,
__stdout__,
__stderr__
> Original values of stdin, stderr, and stdout at program start (e.g., for restores as a last resort; normally, when assigning to sys.stdout, etc., save the old value and restore it in a finally clause). Can be None for GUI apps on Windows with no console.

tracebacklimit
> Maximum number of traceback levels to print on uncaught exceptions; defaults to 1,000 unless assigned.

version
> String containing the version number of the Python interpreter.

version_info

Tuple containing five version identification components: major, minor, micro, release level, and serial. For Python 3.0.1, this is `(3, 0, 1, 'final', 0)` (see the Python Library Reference).

winver

Version number used to form registry keys on Windows platforms (available only on Windows; see the Python Library Reference).

The string Module

The `string` module defines constants and variables for processing string objects. See also the section "Strings" on page 19 for a discussion of the string template substitution and formatting tools `Template` and `Formatter` defined in this module.

Module Functions and Classes

As of Python 2.0, most functions in this module are also available as methods of string objects, and method-based calls are preferred and are more efficient. See the section "Strings" on page 19 for more details and a list of all available string methods not repeated here. Only items unique to the `string` module are listed in this section.

capwords(s)

Split the argument into words using `split`, capitalize each word using `capitalize`, and join the capitalized words using `join`. Replaces runs of whitespace characters by a single space, and removes leading and trailing whitespace.

maketrans(from, to)

Returns a translation table suitable for passing to `bytes.translate`, that will map each character in `from` into the character at the same position in `to`; `from` and `to` must have the same length.

Formatter

    Class that allows creation of custom formatters using the same mechanism as the `str.format()` method described in section "Strings" on page 19.

Template

    String template substitution class (see the section "Strings" on page 19).

Constants

ascii_letters

    The string `ascii_lowercase` + `ascii_uppercase`.

ascii_lowercase

    The string `'abcdefghijklmnopqrstuvwxyz'`; not locale-dependent and will not change.

ascii_uppercase

    The string `'ABCDEFGHIJKLMNOPQRSTUVWXYZ'`; not locale-dependent and will not change.

digits

    The string `'0123456789'`.

hexdigits

    The string `'0123456789abcdefABCDEF'`.

octdigits

    The string `'01234567'`.

printable

    Combination of `digits`, `ascii_letters`, `punctuation`, and `whitespace`.

punctuation

    String of characters that are considered punctuation characters in the locale.

whitespace

    String containing space, tab, linefeed, return, formfeed, and vertical tab: `' \t\n\r\v\f'`.

The os System Module

The os module is the primary operating system (OS) services interface. It provides generic OS support and a standard, platform-independent OS interface. The os module includes tools for environments, processes, files, shell commands, and much more. It also includes a nested submodule, os.path, which provides a portable interface to directory processing tools.

Scripts that use os and os.path for systems programming are generally portable across most Python platforms. However, some os exports are not available on all platforms (e.g., fork is available on Unix and Cygwin, but not in the standard Windows version of Python). Because the portability of such calls can change over time, consult the Python Library Reference for platform details.

See also related system modules: glob (filename expansion); tempfile (temporary files); signal (signal handling); socket (networking and IPC); threading (multithreading); queue (thread communication); subprocess (spawned command control); multiprocessing (threading-like API for processes); getopt and optparse (command-line processing); and others.

Administrative Tools

Following are some miscellaneous module-related exports:

error

> An alias for the built-in OSError exception. Raised for os module-related errors. The accompanying value is a pair containing the numeric error code from errno and the corresponding string, as would be printed by the C function perror(). See the module errno in the Python Library Reference for names of the error codes defined by the underlying OS.

> When exceptions are classes, this exception carries two attributes: errno, the value of the C errno variable;

and `strerror`, the corresponding error message from `strerror()`. For exceptions that involve a file pathname (e.g., `chdir()`, `unlink()`), the exception instance also contains the attribute `filename`, the filename passed in.

name

Name of OS-specific modules whose names are copied to the top level of `os` (e.g., `posix`, `nt`, `mac`, `os2`, `ce`, or `java`). See also `platform` in the section "The sys Module" on page 133.

path

Nested module for portable pathname-based utilities. For example, `os.path.split` is a platform-independent directory name tool that internally uses an appropriate platform-specific call.

Portability Constants

This section describes tools for parsing and building directory and search path strings portably. They are automatically set to the appropriate value for the platform on which a script is running.

curdir

String used to represent current directory (e.g., `.` for Windows and POSIX, `:` for Macintosh).

pardir

String used to represent parent directory (e.g., `..` for POSIX, `::` for Macintosh).

sep

String used to separate directories (e.g., `/` for Unix, `\` for Windows, or `:` for Macintosh).

altsep

Alternative separator string or `None` (e.g., `/` for Windows).

extsep

The character that separates the base filename from the extension (e.g., `.`).

pathsep

> Character used to separate search path components, as in the `PATH` and `PYTHONPATH` shell variable settings (e.g., `;` for Windows, `:` for Unix).

defpath

> Default search path used by `os.exec*p*` calls if there is no `PATH` setting in the shell.

linesep

> String used to terminate lines on current platform (e.g., `\n` for POSIX, `\r` for Mac OS, and `\r\n` for Windows). Do not use this when writing lines in text mode files—use the autotranslation of `'\n'`.

Shell Commands

These functions run programs in the underlying operating system. In Python 2.X, this module has `os.popen2/3/4` calls, which have been replaced by `subprocess.Popen` in Python 3.0.

system(cmd)

> Executes a command string `cmd` in a subshell process. Returns the exit status of the spawned process. Unlike `popen`, does not connect to `cmd`'s standard streams via pipes. Hints: add an `&` at the end of `cmd` to run the command in the background on Unix (e.g., `os.system('python main.py &')`); use a DOS `start` command to launch programs easily on Windows (e.g., `os.system('start file.html')`).

startfile(filepathname)

> Starts a file with its associated application. Acts like double-clicking the file in Windows Explorer or giving the filename as an argument to a DOS `start` command (e.g., with `os.system('start path')`). The file is opened in the application with which its extension is associated; the call does not wait, and does not generally pop up a DOS console window. Windows only, new in version 2.0.

```
popen(cmd, mode='r', buffering=None)
```
Opens a pipe to or from the shell command string cmd, to send or capture data. Returns an open file object, which can be used to either read from cmd's standard output stream stdout (mode 'r') or write to cmd's standard input stream stdin (mode 'w'). For example, dirlist = os.popen('ls -l *.py').read() reads the output of a Unix ls command.

cmd is any command string you can type at your system's console or shell prompt. mode can be 'r' or 'w' and defaults to 'r'. buffering is the same as in the built-in open function. cmd runs independently; its exit status is returned by the resulting file object's close method, except that None is returned if exit status is 0 (no errors). Use readline() or iteration to read output line by line.

Python 2.X also has variants popen2, popen3, and popen4 to connect to other streams of the spawned command (e.g., popen2 returns a tuple (child_stdin, child_stdout)). In Python 3.0, these calls are removed; use subprocess.Popen() instead. The subprocess module in version 2.4 and later allows scripts to spawn new processes, connect to their input/output/error pipes, and obtain their return codes. See the Python Library Reference.

```
spawn*(args...)
```
A family of functions for spawning programs and commands. See "Process Control" on page 150, as well as the Python Library Reference for more details. The subprocess module is a generally preferred alternative to these calls.

Environment Tools

These attributes export execution environment and context.

```
environ
```
The shell environment variable dictionary-like object. os.environ['USER'] is the value of variable USER in the shell (equivalent to $USER in Unix and %USER% in DOS).

Initialized on program start-up. Changes made to `os.envi
ron` by key assignment are exported outside Python using
a call to C's **putenv** and are inherited by any processes that
are later spawned in any way, as well as any linked-in C
code.

`putenv(varname, value)`

Sets the shell environment variable named `varname` to the
string `value`. Affects subprocesses started with `system`,
`popen`, `spawnv`, or `fork` and `execv`. Assignment to
`os.environ` keys automatically calls `putenv` (but `putenv`
calls don't update `environ`).

`getcwd()`

Returns the current working directory name as a string.

`chdir(path)`

Changes the current working directory for this process to
`path`, a directory name string. Future file operations are
relative to the new current working directory.

`strerror(code)`

Returns an error message corresponding to `code`.

`times()`

Returns a five-tuple containing elapsed CPU time information for the calling process in floating-point seconds:
(*user-time*, *system-time*, *child-user-time*, *child-system-
time*, *elapsed-real-time*). Also see the section "The time
Module" on page 176.

`umask(mask)`

Sets the numeric `umask` to `mask` and returns the prior value.

`uname()`

Returns OS name tuple of strings: (*systemname*, *nodename*,
release, *version*, *machine*).

File Descriptor Tools

The following functions process files by their descriptors (`fd` is
a file-descriptor integer). `os` module descriptor-based files are
meant for low-level file tasks and are not the same as **stdio**

file objects returned by the built-in **open()** function (though **os.fdopen** and the file object **fileno** method convert between the two). File objects, not descriptors, should normally be used for most file processing.

close(fd)
> Closes file descriptor **fd** (not a file object).

dup(fd)
> Returns duplicate of file descriptor **fd**.

dup2(fd, fd2)
> Copies file descriptor **fd** to **fd2** (close **fd2** first if open).

fdopen(fd [, mode [, bufsize]])
> Returns a built-in file object (**stdio**) connected to file descriptor **fd** (an integer). **mode** and **bufsize** have the same meaning as in the built-in **open()** function (see the section "Built-in Functions" on page 102). A conversion from descriptor-based files to file objects is normally created by the built-in **open()** function. Hint: use **fileobj.fileno** to convert a file object to a descriptor.

fstat(fd)
> Returns status for file descriptor **fd** (like **stat**).

ftruncate(fd, length)
> Truncates the file corresponding to file descriptor **fd** so that it is at most **length** bytes in size.

isatty(fd)
> Returns **1** if file descriptor **fd** is open and connected to a tty(-like) device.

lseek(fd, pos, how)
> Sets the current position of file descriptor **fd** to **pos** (for random access). **how** can be 0 to set the position relative to the start of the file, 1 to set it relative to the current position, or 2 to set it relative to the end.

open(filename, flags [, mode])
> Opens a file descriptor-based file and returns the file descriptor (an integer, not an **stdio** file object). Intended for low-level file tasks only; not the same as the built-in

open() function. mode defaults to 0777 (octal), and the
current umask value is first masked out. flag is a bitmask:
use | to combine both platform-neutral and platform-
specific flag constants defined in the os module (see
Table 18).

pipe()
> See the section "Process Control" on page 150.

read(fd, n)
> Reads at most n bytes from file descriptor fd and returns
> those bytes as a string.

write(fd, str)
> Writes all bytes in string str to file descriptor fd.

Table 18. Sample or-able flags for os.open

O_APPEND	O_EXCL	O_RDONLY	O_TRUNC
O_BINARY	O_NDELAY	O_RDWR	O_WRONLY
O_CREAT	O_NOCTTY	O_RSYNC	
O_DSYNC	O_NONBLOCK	O_SYNC	

File Pathname Tools

The following functions process files by their pathnames
(path is a string pathname of a file). See also the section "The
os.path Module" on page 153. In Python 2.X, this module also
includes temporary file tools that have been replaced with the
tempfile module in Python 3.0.

chdir(path),
getcwd()
> See the section "Environment Tools" on page 144.

chmod(path, mode)
> Changes mode of file path to numeric mode.

chown(path, uid, gid)
> Changes owner/group IDs of path to numeric uid/gid.

link(srcpath, dstpath)
> Creates a hard link to file src, named dst.

`listdir(path)`

Returns a list of names of all the entries in the directory `path`. A fast and portable alternative to the `glob` module and to running shell listing commands with `os.popen`. See also module `glob` for filename expansion.

`lstat(path)`

Like `stat`, but does not follow symbolic links.

`mkfifo(path [, mode])`

Creates a *FIFO* (a named pipe) identified by string `path` with access permission given by numeric `mode` (but does not open it). The default mode is 0666 (octal). The current `umask` value is first masked out from the `mode`. FIFOs are pipes that live in the filesystem and can be opened and processed like regular files. FIFOs exist until deleted.

`mkdir(path [, mode])`

Makes a directory called `path`, with the given `mode`. The default mode is 777 (octal).

`makedirs(path [, mode])`

Recursive directory-creation function. Like `mkdir`, but makes all intermediate-level directories needed to contain the leaf directory. Throws an exception if the leaf directory already exists or cannot be created. `mode` defaults to 0777 (octal).

`readlink(path)`

Returns the path referenced by a symbolic link `path`.

`remove(path)`,
`unlink(path)`

Removes (deletes) the file named `path`. `remove` is identical to `unlink`. See `rmdir` and `removedirs`, discussed in this list, for removing directories.

`removedirs(path)`

Recursive directory-removal function. Similar to `rmdir`, but if the leaf directory is successfully removed, then directories corresponding to the rightmost path segments will be pruned away until either the whole path is consumed or an error is raised. Throws an exception if the leaf directory could not be removed.

`rename(srcpath, dstpath)`

Renames (moves) file `src` to name `dst`.

`renames(oldpath, newpath)`

Recursive directory- or file-renaming function. Like `rename`, but creation of any intermediate directories needed to make the new pathname good is attempted first. After the rename, directories corresponding to the right-most path segments of the old name will be pruned away using `removedirs`.

`rmdir(path)`

Removes (deletes) a directory named `path`.

`stat(path)`

Runs `stat` system call for `path`; returns a tuple of integers with low-level file information (whose items are defined and processed by tools in module `stat`).

`symlink(srcpath, dstpath)`

Creates a symbolic link to file `src`, called `dst`.

`utime(path, (atime, mtime))`

Sets file `path` access and modification times.

`access(path, mode)`

Consult the Python Library Reference or Unix manpages for details.

`walk(top [, topdown=True [, onerror=None]`
`[, followlinks=False]]])`

Generates the filenames in a directory tree by walking the tree either top-down or bottom-up. For each directory in the tree rooted at directory `top` (including `top` itself), yields a three-tuple `(dirpath, dirnames, filenames)`. `dirpath` is a string, the path to the directory. `dirnames` is a list of the names of the subdirectories in `dirpath` (excluding `.` and `..`). `filenames` is a list of the names of the nondirectory files in `dirpath`. Note that the names in the lists do not contain path components. To get a full path (which begins with `top`) to a file or directory in `dirpath`, do `os.path.join(dirpath, name)`.

If optional argument `topdown` is true or not specified, the triple for a directory is generated before the triples for any of its subdirectories (directories are generated top-down). If `topdown` is false, the triple for a directory is generated after the triples for all its subdirectories (directories are generated bottom-up). If optional `onerror` is specified, it should be a function, which will be called with one argument, an `os.error` instance. By default, will not walk down into symbolic links that resolve to directories; set `followlinks` to `True` to visit directories pointed to by symlinks, on systems that support them.

Python 2.X also provides an `os.path.walk()` call with similar tree-walking functionality, using an event-handler function callback instead of a generator. In Python 3.0, `os.path.walk()` is removed due to its redundancy; use `os.walk()` instead. See also module `glob` for filename expansion.

Process Control

The following functions are used to create and manage processes and programs. Refer also to the section "Shell Commands" on page 143 for other ways to start programs and files.

`abort()`
    Sends a `SIGABRT` signal to the current process. On Unix, the default behavior is to produce a core dump; on Windows, the process immediately returns exit code 3.

`execl(path, arg0, arg1,...)`
    Equivalent to `execv(path, (arg0, arg1,...))`.

`execle(path, arg0, arg1,..., env)`
    Equivalent to `execve(path, (arg0, arg1,...), env)`.

`execlp(path, arg0, arg1,...)`
    Equivalent to `execvp(path, (arg0, arg1,...))`.

---

execve(path, args, env)

Like execv, but the env dictionary replaces the shell variable environment. env must map strings to strings.

execvp(path, args)

Like execv(path, args), but duplicates the shell's actions in searching for an executable file in a list of directories. The directory list is obtained from os.environ['PATH'].

execvpe(path, args, env)

A cross between execve and execvp. The directory list is obtained from os.environ['PATH'].

execv(path, args)

Executes the executable file path with the command-line argument args, replacing the current program in this process (the Python interpreter). args can be a tuple or a list of strings, and it starts with the executable's name by convention (argv[0]). This function call never returns, unless an error occurs while starting the new program.

_exit(n)

Exits the process immediately with status n, without performing cleanup. Normally used only in a child process after a fork; the standard way to exit is to call sys.exit(n).

fork()

Spawns a child process (a virtual copy of the calling process, running in parallel); returns 0 in the child and the new child's process ID in the parent. Not available in standard Windows Python, but is available on Windows in Cygwin Python.

getpid(),
getppid()

Returns the process ID of the current (calling) process; getppid() returns the parent process ID.

getuid(),
geteuid()

Returns the process's user ID; geteuid returns the effective user ID.

`kill(pid, sig)`

> Kills the process with ID `pid` by sending signal `sig`. See also the `signal` module for register signal handlers.

`mkfifo(path [, mode])`

> See the section "File Pathname Tools" on page 147 (files used for process synchronization).

`nice(increment)`

> Adds `increment` to process's "niceness" (i.e., lowers its CPU priority).

`pipe()`

> Returns a tuple of file descriptors (`rfd`, `wfd`) for reading and writing a new anonymous (unnamed) pipe. Used for cross-process communication.

`plock(op)`

> Locks program segments into memory. `op` (defined in `<sys./lock.h>`) determines which segments are locked.

`spawnv(mode, path, args)`

> Executes program `path` in a new process, passing the arguments specified in `args` as a command line. `args` can be a list or a tuple. `mode` is a magic operational constant made from the following names: `P_WAIT`, `P_NOWAIT`, `P_NOWAITO`, `P_OVERLAY`, and `P_DETACH`. On Windows, roughly equivalent to a `fork+execv` combination (`fork` is not yet available on standard Windows Python, though `popen` and `system` are). See also the `subprocess` module for more powerful alternatives.

`spawnve(mode, path, args, env)`

> Like `spawnv`, but passes the contents of mapping `env` as the spawned program's shell environment.

`wait()`

> Waits for completion of a child process. Returns a tuple with child's ID and exit status.

`waitpid(pid, options)`

> Waits for child process with ID `pid` to complete. `options` is 0 for normal use, or `os.WNOHANG` to avoid hanging if no child status is available. If `pid` is 0, the request applies to

any child in the process group of the current process. See also the process exit status-check functions documented in the Python Library Reference (e.g., `WEXITSTATUS(status)` to extract the exit code).

The os.path Module

The `os.path` module provides additional file directory pathname-related services and portability tools. This is a nested module: its names are nested in the `os` module within the submodule `os.path` (e.g., the `exists` function is obtained by importing `os` and using `os.path.exists`).

Most functions in this module take an argument `path`, the string directory pathname of a file (e.g., `"C:\dir1\spam.txt"`). Directory paths are generally coded per the platform's conventions and are mapped to the current working directory if lacking a directory prefix. Hint: forward slashes usually work as directory separators on all platforms. In Python 2.X, this module includes an `os.path.walk` tool, which has been replaced by `os.walk` in Python 3.0.

abspath(path)
    Returns a normalized absolute version of `path`. On most platforms, this is equivalent to `normpath(join(os.getcwd(), path))`.

basename(path)
    Same as second half of pair returned by `split(path)`.

commonprefix(list)
    Returns longest path prefix (character by character) that is a prefix of all paths in `list`.

dirname(path)
    Same as first half of pair returned by `split(path)`.

exists(path)
    True if string `path` is the name of an existing file path.

expanduser(path)
    Returns string that is `path` with embedded ~ username expansion done.

expandvars(path)

Returns string that is **path** with embedded **$** environment variables expanded.

getatime(path)

Returns time of last access of **path** (seconds since the epoch).

getmtime(path)

Returns time of last modification of **path** (seconds since the epoch).

getsize(path)

Returns size, in bytes, of file **path**.

isabs(path)

True if string **path** is an absolute path.

isfile(path)

True if string **path** is a regular file.

isdir(path)

True if string **path** is a directory.

islink(path)

True if string **path** is a symbolic link.

ismount(path)

True if string **path** is a mount point.

join(path1 [, path2 [, ...]])

Joins one or more path components intelligently (using platform-specific separator conventions between each part).

normcase(path)

Normalizes case of a pathname. Has no effect on Unix; on case-insensitive filesystems, converts to lowercase; on Windows, also converts / to \.

normpath(path)

Normalizes a pathname. Collapses redundant separators and up-level references; on Windows, converts / to \.

realpath(path)

Returns the canonical path of the specified filename, eliminating any symbolic links encountered in the path.

`samefile(path1, path2)`

> Returns **true** if both pathname arguments refer to the same file or directory.

`sameopenfile(fp1, fp2)`

> Returns **true** if both file objects refer to the same file.

`samestat(stat1, stat2)`

> Returns **true** if both **stat** tuples refer to the same file.

`split(path)`

> Splits **path** into (**head**, **tail**), where **tail** is the last pathname component and **head** is everything leading up to **tail**. Same as tuple (`dirname(path)`, `basename(path)`).

`splitdrive(path)`

> Splits **path** into a pair (`'drive:'`, `tail`) (on Windows).

`splitext(path)`

> Splits **path** into (**root**, **ext**), where the last component of **root** contains no **.**, and **ext** is empty or starts with a **.**.

`walk(path, visitor, data)`

> An alternative to `os.walk` in Python 2.X only. Removed in Python 3.0: use `os.walk`, not `os.path.walk`.

The re Pattern-Matching Module

The **re** module is the standard regular expression-matching interface. Regular expression (RE) patterns are specified as strings. This module must be imported.

Module Functions

`compile(pattern [, flags])`

> Compile an RE **pattern** string into a regular expression object, for later matching. **flags** (combinable by bitwise | operator) include the following available at the top-level of the **re** module:

A or ASCII or (?a)

Makes \w, \W, \b, \B, \s, and \S perform ASCII-only matching instead of full Unicode matching. This is only meaningful for Unicode patterns and is ignored for byte patterns. Note that for backward compatibility, the re.U flag still exists (as well as its synonym re.UNICODE and its embedded counterpart, ?u), but these are redundant in Python 3.0 since matches are Unicode by default for strings (and Unicode matching isn't allowed for bytes).

I or IGNORECASE or (?i)

Case-insensitive matching.

L or LOCALE or (?L)

Makes \w, \W, \b, \B, \s, \S, \d, and \D dependent on the current locale (default is Unicode for Python 3).

M or MULTILINE or (?m)

Matches to each newline, not whole string.

S or DOTALL or (?s)

. matches *all* characters, including newline.

U or UNICODE or (?u)

Makes \w, \W, \b, \B, \s, \S, \d, and \D dependent on Unicode character properties (new in version 2.0, and superfluous in Python 3).

X or VERBOSE or (?x)

Ignores whitespace in the pattern, outside character sets.

match(pattern, string [, flags])

If zero or more characters at start of string match the pattern string, returns a corresponding MatchObject instance, or None if no match. flags as in compile.

search(pattern, string [, flags])

Scans through string for a location matching pattern; returns a corresponding MatchObject instance, or None if no match. flags as in compile.

split(pattern, string [, maxsplit=0])
>   Splits **string** by occurrences of **pattern**. If capturing ( ) are
>   used in **pattern**, occurrences of patterns or subpatterns
>   are also returned.

sub(pattern, repl, string [, count=0])
>   Returns string obtained by replacing the (first count) left-
>   most nonoverlapping occurrences of **pattern** (a string or
>   an RE object) in **string** by **repl**. **repl** can be a string or a
>   function called with a single **MatchObject** argument, which
>   must return the replacement string. **repl** can also include
>   sequence escapes \1, \2, etc., to use substrings that match
>   groups, or \0 for all.

subn(pattern, repl, string [, count=0])
>   Same as **sub** but returns a tuple (new-string, number-of-
>   subs-made).

findall(pattern, string [, flags])
>   Returns a list of strings giving all nonoverlapping matches
>   of **pattern** in **string**. If one or more groups are present in
>   the pattern, returns a list of groups.

finditer(pattern, string [, flags])
>   Returns an iterator over all nonoverlapping matches for
>   the RE pattern in string (match objects).

escape(string)
>   Returns **string** with all nonalphanumeric characters
>   backslashed, such that they can be compiled as a string
>   literal.

Regular Expression Objects

RE objects are returned by the **re.compile** function and have
the following attributes:

flags
>   The **flags** argument used when the RE object was
>   compiled.

groupindex
>   Dictionary of {group-name: group-number} in the pattern.

pattern

> The pattern string from which the RE object was compiled.

```
match(string [, pos [, endpos]]),
search(string [, pos [, endpos]]),
split(string [, maxsplit=0]),
sub(repl, string [, count=0]),
subn(repl, string [, count=0]),
findall(string [, pos[, endpos]]),
finditer(string [, pos[, endpos]])
```

> Same as earlier re module functions, but pattern is implied, and pos and endpos give start/end string indexes for the match.

Match Objects

Match objects are returned by successful match and search operations, and have the following attributes (see the Python Library Reference for additional attributes omitted here).

pos, endpos

> Values of pos and endpos passed to search or match.

re

> RE object whose match or search produced this.

string

> String passed to match or search.

group([g1, g2,...])

> Returns substrings that were matched by parenthesized groups in the pattern. Accepts zero or more group numbers. If one argument, result is the substring that matched the group whose number is passed. If multiple arguments, result is a tuple with one matched substring per argument. If no arguments, returns entire matching substring. If any group number is 0, return value is entire matching string; otherwise, returns string matching corresponding parenthesized group number in pattern (1...N, from left to

right). Group number arguments can also be group names.

groups()

Returns a tuple of all groups of the match; groups not participating in the match have a value of None.

groupdict()

Returns a dictionary containing all the named subgroups of the match, keyed by the subgroup name.

start([group]), end([group])

Indexes of start and end of substring matched by group (or entire matched string, if no group). If match object M, M.string[M.start(g):M.end(g)]==M.group(g).

span([group])

Returns the tuple (start(group), end(group)).

expand(template)

Returns the string obtained by doing backslash substitution on the template string template, as done by the sub method. Escapes such as \n are converted to the appropriate characters, and numeric back-references (\1, \2) and named back-references (\g<1>, \g<name>) are replaced by the corresponding group.

Pattern Syntax

Pattern strings are specified by concatenating forms (see Table 19), as well as by character class escapes (see Table 20). Python character escapes (e.g., \t for tab) can also appear. Pattern strings are matched against text strings, yielding a Boolean match result, as well as grouped substrings matched by subpatterns in parentheses:

```
>>> import re
>>> patt = re.compile('hello[ \t]*(.*)')
>>> mobj = patt.match('hello   world!')
>>> mobj.group(1)
'world!'
```

In Table 19, *C* is any character, *R* is any regular expression form in the left column of the table, and *m* and *n* are integers. Each form usually consumes as much of the string being matched as possible, except for the nongreedy forms (which consume as little as possible, as long as the entire pattern still matches the target string).

Table 19. Regular expression pattern syntax

Form	Description
.	Matches any character (including newline if DOTALL flag is specified).
^	Matches start of string (of every line in MULTILINE mode).
$	Matches end of string (of every line in MULTILINE mode).
C	Any nonspecial character matches itself.
R*	Zero or more occurrences of preceding regular expression R (as many as possible).
R+	One or more occurrences of preceding regular expression R (as many as possible).
R?	Zero or one occurrence of preceding regular expression R.
R{m}	Matches exactly m repetitions of preceding regular expression R.
R{m,n}	Matches from m to n repetitions of preceding regular expression R.
R*?, R+?, R??, R{m,n}?	Same as *, +, and ?, but matches as few characters/times as possible; *nongreedy*.
[...]	Defines character set; e.g., [a-zA-Z] matches all letters (also see Table 20).

Form	Description
`[^...]`	Defines complemented character set: matches if character is not in set.
`\`	Escapes special characters (e.g., `*?+|()`) and introduces special sequences (see Table 20). Due to Python rules, write as `\\` or `r'\\'`.
`\\`	Matches a literal `\`; due to Python string rules, write as `\\\\` in pattern, or `r'\\'`.
`\number`	Matches the contents of the group of the same number: `(.+) \1` matches "42 42"
`R|R`	Alternative: matches left or right R.
`RR`	Concatenation: matches both Rs.
`(R)`	Matches any RE inside `()`, and delimits a group (retains matched substring).
`(?: R)`	Same as `(R)` but doesn't delimit a group.
`(?= R)`	Look-ahead assertion: matches if R matches next, but doesn't consume any of the string (e.g., `X (?=Y)` matches X if followed by Y).
`(?! R)`	Negative look-ahead assertion: matches if R doesn't match next. Negative of `(?=R)`.
`(?P<name> R)`	Matches any RE inside `()` and delimits a named group (e.g., `r'(?P<id>[a-zA-Z_]\ w*)'` defines a group named `id`).

Form	Description
(?P=name)	Matches whatever text was matched by the earlier group named name.
(?#...)	A comment; ignored.
(?letter)	letter is one of a, i, L, m, s, x, or u. Set flag (re.A, re.I, re.L, etc.) for entire RE.
(?<= R)	Positive look-behind assertion: matches if preceded by a match of fixed-width R.
(?<! R)	Negative look-behind assertion: matches if not preceded by a match of fixed-width R.
(?(id/name)yespattern|nopattern)	Will try to match with yespattern if the group with given id or name exists, else with optional nopattern.

In Table 20, \b, \B, \d, \D, \s, \S, \w, and \W behave differently depending on flags, and defaults to Unicode in Python 3.0, unless ASCII (?a) is used. Tip: use raw strings (r'\n') to literalize backslashes in Table 20 class escapes.

Table 20. Regular expression pattern special sequences

Sequence	Description
\number	Matches text of the group *number* (from 1).
\A	Matches only at the start of the string.
\b	Empty string at word boundaries.

Sequence	Description
\B	Empty string not at word boundary.
\d	Any decimal digit (like [0-9]).
\D	Any nondecimal digit character (like [^0-9]).
\s	Any whitespace character (like [\t\n\r\f\v]).
\S	Any nonwhitespace character (like [^ \t\n\r\f\v]).
\w	Any alphanumeric character.
\W	Any nonalphanumeric character.
\Z	Matches only at the end of the string.

Object Persistence Modules

Three modules comprise the object persistence interface.

dbm (anydbm in Python 2.X)
> Key-based string-only storage files.

pickle (and cPickle in Python 2.X)
> Serializes an in-memory object to/from file streams.

shelve
> Key-based persistent object stores: pickles objects to/from dbm files.

The shelve module implements persistent object stores. shelve in turn uses the pickle module to convert (serialize) in-memory Python objects to byte-stream strings and the dbm module to store serialized byte-stream strings in access-by-key files.

dbm and shelve Modules

dbm is an access-by-key filesystem: strings are stored and fetched by their string keys. The dbm module selects the keyed-access file implementation in your Python interpreter and presents a dictionary-like API for scripts. A persistent object shelve is used like a simple *dbm* file, except that the dbm module is replaced by shelve, and the stored **value** can be almost any kind of Python object (though keys are still strings). In most respects, dbm files and shelves work like dictionaries that must be opened before use, and closed after making changes; all mapping operations and some dictionary methods work.

```
import shelve,
import dbm
```
Gets whatever dbm support library is available: dbm.bsd, dbm.gnu, dbm.ndbm, or dbm.dumb.

```
open(…)
    file = shelve.open(filename
       [, flag='c'
       [, protocol=None
       [, writeback=False]]])
    file = dbm.open(filename
       [, flag='r'
       [, mode]])
```

Creates a new or opens an existing `dbm` file.

`flag` is the same in `shelve` and `dbm` (`shelve` passes it on to `dbm`). It can be `'r'` to open an existing database for reading only (`dbm` default); `'w'` to open an existing database for reading and writing; `'c'` to create the database if it doesn't exist (`shelve` default); or `'n'`, which will always create a new empty database. The `dbm.dumb` module (used by default in 3.0 if no other library is installed) ignores `flag`—the database is always opened for update and is created if it doesn't exist.

For `dbm`, the optional `mode` argument is the Unix mode of the file, used only when the database has to be created. It defaults to octal 0o666.

For `shelve`, the `protocol` argument is passed on from `shelve` to `pickle`. It gives the pickling protocol number (described ahead) used to store shelved objects; it defaults to 0 in Python 2.6, and to 2 in Python 3.0. By default, changes to objects fetched from shelves are not automatically written back to disk. If the optional `writeback` parameter is set to `True`, all entries accessed are cached in memory, and written back at close time; this makes it easier to mutate mutable entries in the shelve, but can consume memory for the cache, making the close operation slow because all accessed entries are written back.

`file['key'] = value`
> Store: creates or changes the entry for `'key'`. Value is a string for `dbm`, or an arbitrary object for `shelve`.

`value = file['key']`
> Fetch: loads the value for the `'key'` entry. For `shelve`, reconstructs object in memory.

`count = len(file)`
> Size: returns the number of entries stored.

`index = file.keys()`
> Index: fetches the stored keys (can use in a `for` or other iteration context).

`found = 'key' in file (or has_key() in 2.X only)`
> Query: sees if there's an entry for `'key'`.

```
del file['key']
```
Delete: removes the entry for `'key'`.

```
file.close()
```
Manual close; required to flush updates to disk for some underlying dbm interfaces.

pickle Module

The `pickle` interface converts nearly arbitrary in-memory Python objects to/from serialized byte-streams. These byte-streams can be directed to any file-like object that has the expected read/write methods. Unpickling re-creates the original in-memory object (with the same value, but a new identity [address]).

See the prior note about Python 2.X's `cPickle` and Python 3.0's `_pickle` optimized modules. Also see the `makefile` method of socket objects for shipping serialized objects over networks.

Pickling interfaces

```
P = pickle.Pickler(fileobject [, protocol=None])
```
Makes a new pickler, for saving to an output file object.

```
P.dump(object)
```
Writes an object onto the pickler's file/stream.

```
pickle.dump(object, fileobject [, protocol=None])
```
Combination of the previous two: pickles object onto file.

```
string = pickle.dumps(object [, protocol=None])
```
Returns pickled representation of object as a string (a `bytes` string in Python 3.0).

Unpickling interfaces

```
U = pickle.Unpickler(fileobject,
encoding="ASCII", errors="strict")
```
Makes unpickler, for loading from input file object.

```
object = U.load()
```
Reads object from the unpickler's file/stream.

```
object = pickle.load(fileobject,
encoding="ASCII", errors="strict")
```
Combination of the previous two: unpickles object from file.

```
object = pickle.loads(string,
encoding="ASCII", errors="strict")
```
Reads object from a character string (a bytes string in Python 3.0).

Usage notes

- In Python 3.0, files used to store pickled objects should always be opened in binary mode for all protocols, because the pickler produces `bytes` strings, and text mode files do not support writing `bytes` (text mode files encode and decode Unicode text in 3.0).

- In Python 2.6, files used to store pickled objects must be opened in binary mode for all pickle protocols >= 1, to suppress line-end translations in binary pickled data. Protocol 0 is ASCII-based, so its files may be opened in either text or binary mode, as long as they are done so consistently.

- `fileobject` is an open file object, or any object that implements file object attributes called by the interface. `Pickler` calls the file `write` method with a string argument. `Unpickler` calls the file `read` method with a byte-count and `readline` without arguments.

- `protocol` is an optional argument that selects a format for pickled data, available in both the `Pickler` constructor and the module's `dump` and `dumps` convenience functions. This argument takes a value `0...3`, where higher protocol numbers are generally more efficient, but may also be incompatible with unpicklers in earlier Python releases. The default protocol number in Python 3.0 is `3`, which cannot be unpickled by Python 2.X. The default protocol in Python 2.6 is `0`, which is less efficient but most portable. Protocol `-1` automatically uses the highest protocol supported. When unpickling, protocol is implied by pickled data contents.

- The unpickler's `encoding` and `errors` optional keyword-only arguments are available in Python 3.0 only. They are used to decode 8-bit string instances pickled by Python 2.X. These default to `'ASCII'` and `'strict'`, respectively.

- `Pickler` and `Unpickler` are exported classes that may be customized by subclassing. See the Python Library Reference for available methods.

The tkinter GUI Module and Tools

`tkinter` (named `Tkinter` in Python 2.X, and a module package in Python 3.0) is a portable graphical user interface (GUI) construction library shipped with Python as a standard library module. `tkinter` provides an object-based interface to the open source Tk library and implements native look and feel for Python-coded GUIs on Windows, X-Windows, and Mac OS. It is portable, simple to use, well documented, widely used, mature, and well supported. Other portable GUI options for Python such as *wxPython* and *PyQT* are third-party extensions with richer widget sets but generally more complex coding requirements.

tkinter Example

In `tkinter` scripts, *widgets* are customizable classes (e.g., `Button`, `Frame`), *options* are keyword arguments (e.g., `text="press"`), and *composition* refers to object embedding, not pathnames (e.g., `Label(top,...)`):

```
from tkinter import *          # widgets, constants

def msg():                     # callback handler
    print('hello stdout...')

top = Frame()                  # make a container
top.pack()
Label(top,  text="Hello world").pack(side=TOP)
```

```
widget = Button(top, text="press", command=msg)
widget.pack(side=BOTTOM)
top.mainloop()
```

tkinter Core Widgets

Table 21 lists the primary widget classes in the **tkinter** module.
These are true Python classes that can be subclassed and embedded in other objects. To create a screen device, make
an instance of the corresponding class, configure it, and ar-
range it with one of the geometry manager interface methods
(e.g., `Button(text='hello').pack()`). In addition to Table 21's
classes, the **tkinter** module provides a large set of predefined
names (a.k.a. constants) used to configure widgets (e.g., RIGHT,
BOTH, YES); these are automatically loaded from
tkinter.constants (Tkconstants in Python 2.X).

Table 21. Module tkinter core widget classes

Widget class	Description
Label	Simple message area
Button	Simple labeled pushbutton widget
Frame	Container for attaching and arranging other widget objects
Toplevel, Tk	Top-level windows managed by the window manager
Message	Multiline text-display field (label)
Entry	Simple single-line text entry field
Checkbutton	Two-state button widget, used for multiple-choice selections
Radiobutton	Two-state button widget, used for single-choice selections
Scale	A slider widget with scalable positions
PhotoImage	Image object for placing full-color images on other widgets
BitmapImage	Image object for placing bitmap images on other widgets
Menu	Options associated with a Menubutton or top-level window
Menubutton	Button that opens a Menu of selectable options/submenus
Scrollbar	Bar for scrolling other widgets (e.g., Listbox, Canvas, Text)
Listbox	List of selection names

Widget class	Description
Text	Multiline text browse/edit widget, support for fonts, etc.
Canvas	Graphics drawing area: lines, circles, photos, text, etc.
OptionMenu	*Composite*: pull-down selection list
PanedWindow	A multipane window interface
LabelFrame	A labeled frame widget
Spinbox	A multiple selection widget
ScrolledText	Python 2.X name (available in module tkinter.scrolled text in Python 3.0); *Composite*: text with attached scrollbar
Dialog	Python 2.X name (available in module tkinter.dialog in Python 3.0); *Old*: common dialog maker (see newer common dialog calls in the next section)

Common Dialog Calls

Module tkinter.messagebox (tkMessageBox in Python 2.X)

```
showinfo(title=None, message=None, **options)
showwarning(title=None, message=None, **options)
showerror(title=None, message=None, **options)
askquestion(title=None, message=None, **options)
askokcancel(title=None, message=None, **options)
askyesno(title=None, message=None, **options)
askretrycancel(title=None, message=None, **options)
```

Module tkinter.simpledialog (tkSimpleDialog in Python 2.X)

```
askinteger(title, prompt, **kw)
askfloat(title, prompt, **kw)
askstring(title, prompt, **kw)
```

Module tkinter.colorchooser (tkColorChooser in Python 2.X)

```
askcolor(color = None, **options)
```

Module tkinter.filedialog (tkFileDialog in Python 2.X)

```
class Open
class SaveAs
class Directory
```

```
askopenfilename(**options)
asksaveasfilename(**options)
askopenfile(mode="r", **options)
asksaveasfile(mode="w", **options)
askdirectory(**options)
```

The common dialog call options are **defaultextension** (added to filename if not explicitly given), **filetypes** (sequence of (**label, pattern**) tuples), **initialdir** (initial directory, remembered by classes), **initialfile** (initial file), **parent** (window in which to place the dialog box), and **title** (dialog box title).

Additional tkinter Classes and Tools

Table 22 lists some commonly used tkinter interfaces and tools beyond the core widget class and standard dialog set.

Table 22. Additional tkinter tools

Tool category	Available tools
tkinter linked-variable classes	StringVar, IntVar, DoubleVar, BooleanVar (in tkinter module)
Geometry management methods	pack, grid, place widget object methods, plus configuration options in module
Scheduled callbacks	Widget after, wait, and update methods; file I/O callbacks
Other tkinter tools	Clipboard access; bind/Event low-level event processing widget object methods; widget config options; modal dialog box support
tkinter extensions (search the Web)	*PMW*: more widgets; *PIL*: images; tree widgets, font support, drag-and-drop, tix widgets, ttk themed widgets, etc.

Tcl/Tk-to-Python/tkinter Mappings

Table 23 compares Python's **tkinter** API to the base Tk library as exposed by the Tcl language. In general, Tcl's command strings map to objects in the Python language. Specifically, in Python's **tkinter**, the Tk GUI interface differs from Tcl in the following ways:

Creation

Widgets are created as class instance objects by calling a widget class.

Masters (parents)

Parents are previously created objects, passed to widget class constructors.

Widget options

Options are constructor or `config` keyword arguments, or indexed keys.

Operations

Widget operations (actions) become **tkinter** widget class object methods.

Callbacks

Callback handlers are any callable object: function, method, `lambda`, class with __call__ method, etc.

Extension

Widgets are extended using Python class inheritance mechanisms.

Composition

Interfaces are constructed by attaching objects, not by concatenating names.

Linked variables

Variables associated with widgets are **tkinter** class objects with methods.

Table 23. Tk-to-tkinter mappings

Operation	Tcl/Tk	Python/tkinter
Creation	frame .panel	panel = Frame()
Masters	button .panel.quit	quit = Button(panel)
Options	button .panel.go -fg black	go = Button(panel, fg='black')
Configure	.panel.go config -bg red	go.config(bg='red') go['bg'] = 'red'

Operation	Tcl/Tk	Python/tkinter
Actions	`.popup invoke`	`popup.invoke()`
Packing	`pack .panel -side left -fill x`	`panel.pack(side=LEFT, fill=X)`

Internet Modules and Tools

This section summarizes Python's support for Internet scripting.

Commonly Used Library Modules

Following are summaries of some of the more commonly used modules in the Python Internet modules set. This is just a representative sample; see the Python Library Reference for a more complete list.

socket

> Low-level network communications support (TCP/IP, UDP, etc.). Interfaces for sending and receiving data over BSD-style sockets: `socket.socket()` makes an object with socket call methods (e.g., `object.bind()`). Most protocol and server modules use this module internally.

socketserver (SocketServer in Python 2.X)

> Framework for general threading and forking network servers.

xdrlib

> Encodes binary data portably (also see socket modules earlier in this list).

select

> Interfaces to Unix and Windows select function. Waits for activity on one of N files or sockets. Commonly used to multiplex among multiple streams or to implement timeouts. Works only for sockets on Windows, not files.

`cgi`

> Server-side CGI script support: `cgi.FieldStorage` parses the input stream; `cgi.escape` applies HTML escape conventions to output streams. To parse and access form information: after a CGI script calls `form=cgi.FieldStorage()`, `form` is a dictionary-like object with one entry per form field (e.g., `form["name"].value` is form field `name` text).

`urllib.request` (`urllib`, `urllib2` in Python 2.X)

> Fetches web pages and server script outputs from their Internet addresses (URLs): `urllib.request.urlopen(`*url*`)` returns file with `read` methods; also `urllib.request.urlretrieve(`*remote*, *local*`)`. Supports HTTP, FTP, gopher, and local file URLs.

`urllib.parse` (`urlparse` in Python 2.X)

> Parses URL string into components. Also contains tools for escaping URL text: `urllib.parse.quote_plus(`*str*`)` does URL escapes for text inserted into HTML output streams.

`ftplib`

> FTP (file transfer protocol) modules. *ftplib* provides interfaces for Internet file transfers in Python programs. After *ftp=ftplib.FTP(*`'sitename'`*)*, `ftp` has methods for login, changing directories, fetching/storing files and listings, etc. Supports binary and text transfers; works on any machine with Python and an Internet connection.

`poplib`, `imaplib`, `smtplib`

> POP, IMAP (mail fetch), and SMTP (mail send) protocol modules.

`email` *package*

> Parses and constructs email messages with headers and attachments. Also contains MIME support.

`http.client` (`httplib` in Python 2), `nntplib`, `telnetlib`

> HTTP (web), NNTP (news), and Telnet protocol client modules.

`http.server` (`CGIHTTPServer` and `SimpleHTTPServer` in Python 2.X)
> HTTP request server implementations.

`xml` package, `html` package (`htmllib` in Python 2.X)
> Parse MXML documents and HTML web page contents. `xml` package supports DOM, SAX, and ElementTree parsing models.

`xmlrpc` package (`xmlrpclib` in Python 2.X)
> XML-RPC remote method call protocol.

`uu`, `binhex`, `base64`, `binascii`, `quopri`
> Encodes and decodes binary (or other) data transmitted as text.

Table 24 lists some of these modules by protocol type.

Table 24. Selected Python Internet modules by protocol

Protocol	Common function	Port number	Python module
HTTP	Web pages	80	`http.client,` `urllib.request, xmlrpc.*`
NNTP	Usenet news	119	`nntplib`
FTP data default	File transfers	20	`ftplib, urllib.request`
FTP control	File transfers	21	`ftplib, urllib.request`
SMTP	Sending email	25	`smtplib`
POP3	Fetching email	110	`poplib`
IMAP4	Fetching email	143	`imaplib`
Telnet	Command lines	23	`telnetlib`

Other Standard Library Modules

This section documents a handful of additional standard library modules. See the Python Library Reference for details on all built-in tools, and the PyPI websites (described in "Assorted

Hints" on page 187) or your favorite web search engine for third-party modules and tools.

The math Module

The math module exports C standard math library tools for use in Python. Table 25 lists this module's exports; see the Python Library Reference for more details. Also see the cmath module in the Python library for complex number tools and the *NumPy* system for advanced numeric work.

Table 25. math module exports in Python 3.0 and 2.6

acos	acosh	asin	asinh	atan
atan2	atanh	ceil	copysign	cos
cosh	degrees	e	exp	fabs
factorial	floor	fmod	frexp	fsum
hypot	isinf	isnan	ldexp	log
log10	log1p	modf	pi	pow
radians	sin	sinh	sqrt	tan
tanh	trunc			

The time Module

Following is a partial list of time module exports. See the Python Library Reference for more details.

clock()
> Returns the CPU time or real time since the start of the process or since the first call to clock(). Precision and semantics is platform-dependent (see Python manuals). Returns seconds expressed as a floating-point number. Useful for benchmarking and timing alternative code sections.

ctime(secs)
> Converts a time expressed in seconds since the epoch to a string representing local time (e.g., ctime(time())). The

argument is optional and defaults to the current time if omitted.

`time()`

Returns a floating-point number representing UTC time in seconds since the epoch. On Unix, epoch is 1970. May have better precision than `clock()` on some platforms (see Python manuals).

`sleep(secs)`

Suspends the process's (calling thread's) execution for `secs` seconds. `secs` can be a float to represent fractions of seconds.

The datetime Module

Tools for subtracting dates, adding days to dates, and so on. See the Python Library Reference for details.

```
>>> from datetime import date, timedelta
>>> date(2009, 12, 17) - date(2009, 11, 29)
datetime.timedelta(18)

>>> date(2009, 11, 29) + timedelta(18)
datetime.date(2009, 12, 17)
```

Threading Modules

Threads are lightweight processes that share global memory (i.e., lexical scopes and interpreter internals) and all run in parallel within the same process. Python thread modules work portably across platforms.

`_thread` (named `thread` in Python 2.X)

Python's basic and low-level thread interface module. Tools to start, stop, and synchronize functions run in parallel. To spawn a thread: `_thread.start_new_thread(function, argstuple)`. Function `start_new_thread` is a synonym for `start_new` (which is documented as obsolete in 3.0). To synchronize threads, use thread locks: `lock=thread.allocate_lock()`; `lock.acquire()`; *update-objects*; `lock.release()`.

`threading`
> Module `threading` builds upon `thread`, to provide customizable threading-oriented classes: `Thread`, `Condition`, `Semaphore`, `Lock`, etc. Subclass `Thread` to overload `run` action method. This is more powerful than `_thread`, but also requires more code in simpler use cases.

`queue` (named `Queue` in Python 2.X)
> A multiproducer, multiconsumer FIFO queue of objects implementation, especially useful for threaded applications (see the Python Library Reference). Locks `get` and `put` operations to synchronize access to data on the queue.

Binary Data Parsing

The `struct` module provides an interface for parsing and constructing packed binary data as strings. Commonly used in conjunction with the `rb` and `wb` binary-mode file open modes. See the Python Library Reference for format datatype and endian codes.

`string = struct.pack(format, v1, v2, ...)`
> Returns a string (a `bytes` in 3.0 and a `str` in 2.6) containing the values `v1`, `v2`, etc., packed according to the given format string. The arguments must match the values required by the format's type codes exactly. The format string can specify the endian format of the result in its first character, as well as repeat counts for individual type codes.

`tuple = struct.unpack(format, string)`
> Unpacks the string (a `bytes` in 3.0 and a `str` in 2.6) according to the given format string.

`struct.calcsize(fmt)`
> Returns size of the `struct` (and hence of the string) corresponding to the given format.

Following is an example showing how to pack and unpack data using `struct` in Python 3.0 (Python 2 uses normal `str` strings instead of `bytes`):

```
>>> import struct
>>> data = struct.pack('4si', 'spam', 123)
>>> data
b'spam{\x00\x00\x00'
>>> x, y = struct.unpack('4si', data)
>>> x, y
(b'spam', 123)

>>> open('data', 'wb').write(struct.pack('>if', 1, 2.0))
8
>>> open('data', 'rb').read()
b'\x00\x00\x00\x01@\x00\x00\x00'

>>> struct.unpack('>if', open('data', 'rb').read())
(1, 2.0)
```

Python Portable SQL Database API

Python's portable SQL database API provides script portability between different vendor-specific SQL database packages. For each vendor, install the vendor-specific extension module, but write your scripts according to the portable database API. Your database scripts will largely continue working unchanged after migrating to a different underlying vendor package.

Note that most database extension modules are not part of the Python standard library; they must be fetched and installed separately. The SQLite embedded in-process relational database package is included with Python as standard library module **sqlite3**, intended for program data storage and prototyping. See also the section "Object Persistence Modules" on page 163 for simpler storage alternatives.

API Usage Example

The following uses the SQLite standard library module. Usage for enterprise-level database such as MySQL, PostgreSQL, and Oracle are similar, but require different connection parameters and installation of extension modules:

```
>>> from sqlite3 import connect
>>> conn = connect(r'C:\users\mark\misc\temp.db')
>>> curs = conn.cursor()

>>> curs.execute('create table jobs (name, title, pay)')
>>> prefix = 'insert into jobs values '
>>> curs.execute(prefix + "('Bob', 'dev', 100)")
>>> curs.execute(prefix + "('Sue', 'dev', 120)")

>>> curs.execute("select * from jobs where pay > 100")
>>> for (name, title, pay) in curs.fetchall():
...     print(name, title, pay)
...
Sue dev 120

>>> curs.execute("select name, pay from jobs").fetchall()
[('Bob', 100), ('Sue', 120)]

>>> query = "select * from jobs where title = ?"
>>> curs.execute(query, ('dev',)).fetchall()
[('Bob', 'dev', 100), ('Sue', 'dev', 120)]
```

Module Interface

This and the following sections provide a *partial* list of exports; see the full API specification at *http://www.python.org* for details omitted here.

connect(parameters...)

>   Constructor for connection objects; represents a connection to the database. Parameters are vendor-specific.

paramstyle

>   String giving type of parameter marker formatting (e.g., **qmark = ?** style).

Warning

>   Exception raised for important warnings such as data truncations.

Error

>   Exception that is the base class of all other error exceptions.

Connection Objects

Connection objects respond to the following methods:

close()
: Closes the connection now (rather than when __del__ is called).

commit()
: Commits any pending transactions to the database.

rollback()
: Rolls database back to the start of any pending transaction; closing a connection without committing the changes first will cause an implicit rollback.

cursor()
: Returns a new cursor object for submitting SQL strings through the connection.

Cursor Objects

Cursor objects represent database cursors, used to manage the context of a fetch operation.

description
: Sequence of seven-item sequences; each contains information describing one result column: (*name*, *type_code*, *display_size*, *internal_size*, *precision*, *scale*, *null_ok*).

rowcount
: Specifies the number of rows that the last execute* produced (for DQL statements like select) or affected (for DML statements like update or insert).

callproc(procname [,parameters])
: Calls a stored database procedure with the given name. The sequence of parameters must contain one entry for each argument that the procedure expects; result is returned as a modified copy of the inputs.

`close()`

    Closes the cursor now (rather than when `__del__` is called).

`execute(operation [,parameters])`

    Prepares and executes a database operation (query or command); parameters can be specified as a list of tuples to insert multiple rows in a single operation (but `executemany` is preferred).

`executemany(operation, seq_of_parameters)`

    Prepares a database operation (query or command) and executes it against all parameter sequences or mappings in sequence `seq_of_parameters`. Similar to multiple `execute` calls.

`fetchone()`

    Fetches the next row of a query result set, returning a single sequence, or `None` when no more data is available.

`fetchmany([size=cursor.arraysize])`

    Fetches the next set of rows of a query result, returning a sequence of sequences (e.g., a list of tuples). An empty sequence is returned when no more rows are available.

`fetchall()`

    Fetches all (remaining) rows of a query result, returning them as a sequence of sequences (e.g., a list of tuples).

Type Objects and Constructors

`Date(year,month,day)`

    Constructs an object holding a date value.

`Time(hour,minute,second)`

    Constructs an object holding a time value.

`None`

    SQL NULL values are represented by the Python `None` on input and output.

Python Idioms and Hints

This section lists common Python coding tricks and general usage hints. Consult the Python Library Reference and Python Language Reference (*http://www.python.org/doc/*) for further information on topics mentioned here.

Core Language Hints

- `S[:]` makes a top-level (shallow) copy of any sequence; `copy.deepcopy(X)` makes full copies; `list(L)` and `D.copy()` copy lists and dictionaries.

- `L[:0]=[X,Y,Z]` inserts items at front of list L, in-place.

- `L[len(L):]=[X,Y,Z]`, `L.extend([X,Y,Z])`, and `L += [X,Y,Z]` all insert multiple items at the end of a list, in-place.

- `L.append(X)` and `X=L.pop()` can be used to implement in-place stack operations, where the end of the list is the top of the stack.

- Use `for key in D.keys():` to iterate through dictionaries, or simply `for key in D:` in version 2.2 and later. In Python 3.0 these two forms are equivalent, since `keys` is an iterable view.

- Use `for key in sorted(D):` to iterate over dictionary keys in sorted fashion in version 2.4 and later; the form `K=D.keys(); K.sort(); for key in K:` also works in Python 2.X but not Python 3.0, since `keys` results are view objects, not lists.

- `X=A or B or None` assigns X to the first true object among A and B, or `None` if both are false (i.e., 0 or empty).

- `X,Y = Y,X` swaps the values of X and Y.

- `red, green, blue = range(3)` assigns integer series.

- Use `try/finally` statements to ensure that arbitrary termination code is run; especially useful around locking calls (acquire before the `try`, release in the `finally`).

- Use `with`/`as` statements to guarantee that object-specific termination code is run; for objects that support the context manager protocol (e.g., file auto-close, tread lock auto-release).

- Wrap iterables in a `list()` call to view all their results interactively in Python 3; this includes `range()`, `map()`, `zip()`, `filter()`, `dict.keys()`, and more.

Environment Hints

- Use `if __name__ == '__main__':` to add self-test code or a call to a main function at the bottom of module files; true only when file is run, not when it is imported as a library component.

- To load file contents in a single expression, use `data=open('filename').read()`.

- To iterate through text files by lines, use `for line in file:` in version 2.2 and later (in older versions, use `for line in file.readlines():`).

- To retrieve command-line arguments, use `sys.argv`.

- To retrieve shell environment settings, use `os.environ`.

- The standard streams are: `sys.stdin`, `sys.stdout`, and `sys.stderror`.

- To return a list of files matching a given pattern, use: `glob.glob('pattern')`.

- To return a list of files and subdirectories on a path, use: `os.listdir('.')`.

- To walk an entire tree of directories, use `os.walk` in Python 3.0 and 2.6 (`os.path.walk` is also available in Python 2.6 only).

- To run shell commands within Python scripts, you can use `os.system('cmdline')`, `output=os.popen('cmdline', 'r').read()`. The latter form reads the spawned program's standard output, and may also be used to read line-by-line.

- Other streams of a spawned command are available via the `subprocess` module in Python 3.0, and the `os.popen2/3/4` calls in Python 2.X only. The `os.fork/os.exec*` calls have similar effect on Unix-like platforms.

- To make a file an executable script on Unix-like platforms, add a line like `#!/usr/bin/env python` or `#!/usr/local/bin/python` at the top and give the file executable permissions with a `chmod` command. On Windows, files can be clicked and run directly due to the registry.

- The `dir([object])` function is useful for inspecting attribute namespaces; `print(object.__doc__)` often gives documentation.

- The `help([object])` function provides interactive help for modules, functions, types, and more; `help(str)` gives help on the `str` type; `help("module")` gives help on modules even if they have not yet been imported; and `help("topic")` gives help on keywords and other help topics (use `"topics"` for a list of help topics).

- `print()` and `input()` (known as `print` and `raw_input()` in Python 2.X) use `sys.stdout` and `sys.stdin` streams: assign to file-like objects to redirect I/O internally, or use the `print(..., file=F)` form in Python 3.0 (or the `print >> F, ...` form in Python 2.X).

Usage Hints

- Use `from __future__ import` *featurename* to enable experimental language features that might break existing code.

- Intuition about performance in Python programs is usually wrong: always measure before optimizing or migrating to C. Use the `profile` and `time` modules (as well as *cProfile* and *timeit*).

- See modules `unittest` (a.k.a. *PyUnit*) and `doctest` for automated testing tools shipped with the Python standard library; `unittest` is a class framework; `doctest` scans documentation strings for tests and outputs.

- See the **pydoc** library module and script shipped with Python for extraction and display of documentation strings associated with modules, functions, classes, and methods.

- See the section "Warnings Framework" on page 130, as well as -W in the section "Command-Line Options" on page 4, for details about turning off future-deprecation warnings emitted by the interpreter.

- See *Distutils*, *PyInstaller*, *py2exe*, *eggs*, and other tools for Python program distribution options.

- See *PyInstaller* and *py2exe* for turning Python programs into *.exe* files for Windows.

- See *NumPy*, *SciPy*, and related packages for extensions that turn Python into a numeric-scientific-programming tool with vector objects, etc.

- See *ZODB* and others for full-featured OODB support that allows Python native objects to be stored by key, and *SQLObject*, *SQLAlchemy*, and others for object relational mappers that allow classes to be used with relational tables.

- See *SWIG* (among others) for a tool that can automatically generate glue code for using C and C++ libraries within Python scripts.

- See *IDLE* for a development GUI shipped with Python, with syntax-coloring text editors, object browsers, debugging, etc.; see also *PythonWin*, *Komodo*, *Eclipse*, *NetBeans*, and others for additional IDE options.

- See *Emacs* help for tips on editing/running code in the Emacs text editor. Most other editors support Python as well (e.g., auto-indenting, coloring), including *VIM* and *IDLE*; see the editors' page at *www.python.org*.

- Porting to Python 3.0: use the -3 command-line option in Python 2.6 to issue incompatibility warnings, and see the *2to3* script which automatically converts much 2.X code to run under 3.X Python.

Assorted Hints

- Important websites to refer to:

  http://www.python.org
  > The Python home page

  http://oreilly.com
  > The publisher's home page

  http://www.python.org/pypi
  > Additional third-party Python tools

  http://www.rmi.net/~lutz
  > The author's site

- Python philosophy: `import this`.

- You should say `spam` and `eggs` instead of `foo` and `bar` in Python examples.

- Always look on the bright side of life.

Index

A

abs function, 102
all function, 102
any function, 102
apply function (Python 2.6),
        119
arguments, command line, 6
ArithmeticError class, 125
as clauses, 71, 72, 81
ascii function, 102
assert statement, 80
AssertionError class, 125
assignment statement, 57
AttributeError class, 125
attributes, 83, 85
        built-in, 131
        pseudo-private, 86
augmented assignments, 57
augmented binary methods,
        96

B

-b Python option, 4
-B Python option, 4
backslash escape sequences,
        19
base classes, 74
BaseException class, 124
basestring function (Python
        2.6), 120
bin function, 102
binary data encoding, 34
binary methods, 94
blocks, 53
bool function, 102
Boolean operations, 11
Boolean type, 52
break statement, 63
buffer function (Python 2.6),
        120
buffering, 112
built-in attributes, 131
built-in exceptions, 124–131

We'd like to hear your suggestions for improving our indexes. Send email to
index@oreilly.com.
